Allen Eyles is the
film histories, inclu
Brothers: Their Worl
the Movies (1976),
Harrison (1985), as well as
Sherlock Holmes: A Centenary Celebration (1986), and *That Was Hollywood The 1930s* (1987).

Allen Eyles was formerly the editor of the magazines *Focus on Film* and *Films and Filming* and in his spare time currently edits *Picture House* magazine.

He lives with his wife, daughter and two cats in Croydon.

HUMPHREY
BOGART

Allen Eyles

SPHERE BOOKS LIMITED

A Sphere Book

First published in Great Britain in 1975 in
The Movie Makers series by Macmillan Publishers, London

This revised, expanded edition first published in Great Britain
by Sphere Books Limited

ISBN 0 7474 0647 2

Photoset in North Wales by
Derek Doyle & Associates, Mold, Clwyd
Printed in Great Britain by
BPCC Hazell Books
Aylesbury, Bucks, England
Member of BPCC Ltd.

Sphere Books Ltd
A Division of
Macdonald & Co (Publishers) Ltd
Orbit House
1 New Fetter Lane
London EC4A 1AR

A Member of Maxwell Macmillan Pergamon Publishing Corporation

CONTENTS

CONTENTS

ACKNOWLEDGEMENTS

The author gratefully acknowledges the assistance of Pat Billings, Jeremy Boulton, Peter Carr, Peter Emerson, Peter Haigh, Charles L. Hoyt, Philip Jenkinson, Alvin H. Marill, David Meeker, Nicky North and David Shipman; and especially my wife, Lesley, for her help in typing the manuscript for this revised edition.

This book is illustrated with publicity photographs mostly obtained from the Stills Library of the National Film Archive, London, and originally issued for promotional use by Fox, Columbia, Warner Bros., United Artists, Romulus, Paramount and unidentified sources.

ACKNOWLEDGEMENTS

The author gratefully acknowledges the assistance of Jill Bailey, Jacky Bagnall, Robert Burton, Terry Cash, Terry Jennings, Ron Freethy, Charles de Flougny, and others, from Heinemann Educational Books and David Shipley, and Susanna Jones to list the help and tribute to the many associated editions.

The book is illustrated with pictures and images obtained from the Skills Library of the Natural History Museum, except where otherwise stated. For permission and assistance we are indebted to the British Museum (Natural History), and to other sources.

1

THE MAKING OF A LEGEND

When Humphrey Bogart died on 14 January 1957, the circumstances gave a sad twist to the news that made headlines around the world. Bogart was barely past his mid-fifties, still active, in great demand, very nearly as popular as he had been in his prime and busily broadening his appeal with more varied roles than before. The loss was not only that of the man but of the films he would have undoubtedly gone on to make.

Then there was the nature of his death. Details of his courageous, painful, protracted battle with cancer – a cancer long hinted at but only publicly confirmed after the announcement of his death – evoked admiration and respect, and attached the screen image of bravery to the man himself. It was obvious, too, that in his private life he had had much to live for, with a young and devoted wife and two small children.

Furthermore, of the great stars who had sprung up in the Thirties and Forties to become Hollywood's 'immortals', Bogart was the first to go. In the years preceding his death, only James Dean's demise had caused an equivalent stir and that was a different matter; otherwise, John Garfield had been the biggest loss but that was much earlier and he was not in Bogart's league. After Bogart, death pounced on Clark Gable, Gary Cooper, Tyrone Power, and Alan Ladd, causing the same jolt of realisation about the mortality of the flesh until their continuing life on celluloid reasserted itself.

Cult figures are usually those that die young – James Dean, Marilyn Monroe and Elvis Presley, so perhaps the perception that Bogart died prematurely contributes to his cult appeal. But there is certainly something about Bogart that has made him immortal, and given his work a timeless appeal. Yet, in any case Bogart *deserves* to be remembered for the uncommonly fine and sensitive actor he was.

Of course, luck played its part. Though stardom came late to Bogart, he was given a large number of great films in which to develop and display his persona to great effect. (The same is true of John Wayne. If Alan Ladd had managed a few more films like *Shane*, if Clark Gable had come up with a few more like *Gone with the Wind* and *It Happened One Night*, then they might match Bogart in terms of popular affection.) Bogart, like John Wayne, was lucky to work with great directors who could make the most of a performer's abilities. In Wayne's case, they were principally John Ford and Howard Hawks. In Bogart's case, they were principally Hawks (*To Have and Have Not, The Big Sleep*), and John Huston (*The Maltese Falcon, The Treasure of the Sierra Madre, The African Queen*). Bogart's contribution to these films (and others, especially *Casablanca*) is an essential part of what makes them great.

The public is very selective about what it responds to, and prizes, from the past. It is the great laughter-makers who, understandably, best endure the passing of time: the Marx Brothers, W.C. Fields, Stan Laurel and Oliver Hardy, Buster Keaton and Charlie Chaplin. But at other times, for other reasons, there is a craving for the fragility of Garbo, the brashness of Cagney, or the stoic heroism of Bogart.

The screen Bogart is usually a man confronted by danger. His many gangster films of the Thirties, in which he usually died in the last reel, forever stamped him as a vulnerable figure. These early criminal roles also marked him as a man of volatile temperament and violent impulses. Many of Bogart's films are concerned as much with inner stress as with outer danger. This neurotic touchiness (in real life, he hated strangers to lay a hand on him), and his aloofness seem to reflect a profound disillusionment, a deep cynicism that the real Bogart felt about his Hollywood surroundings and expressed in his legendary rudeness. Events have made the screen Bogart the way he is, and so, despite his faults, he gains the sympathy of the audience rather than their condemnation.

In the Bogart of the Forties one senses a craving for emotional honesty and deep commitment. He is an idealist who has lost his ideals, a misanthropist in search of a cause, a misogynist awaiting the right woman. Often there are no happy solutions to his problems, only more living to be done with as much style and as little sentimentality as possible. Bogart's is thus an intensely attractive dilemma. He is a model hero for perplexing times.

One reason for his particular effectiveness as a screen performer is his looks. Photographs of Bogart as a Broadway juvenile in his twenties are hard to believe: they show a striking smile, a lean face and well-oiled hair in the Valentino tradition. He had debonair, uncomplicated good looks that suited his lightweight roles in romantic comedy – his scarred upper lip was not noticeable. With his good looks, Bogart went to Hollywood in the early Thirties and vied unsuccessfully with all the other handsome young men who could remember lines, articulate clearly, swing a tennis racket and sip a cocktail.

It was not until *The Petrified Forest* (1936) that he made an impression – an indelible one of a man who had taken a lot of wear and tear. The Bogart face now had 'character', had experienced life and was hardened by most of what it had seen. This was the image Bogart worked on. He played upon his facial aberrations: the twitch in the right cheek at moments of stress or annoyance; the unusually moist lower lip that gleamed under the lights; the watery eyes that also glittered vividly. He told cameramen like James Wong Howe: 'Don't take the lines out of my face. Leave them there.' In *Dark Passage* (1947), he allowed his features to be represented as the outcome of plastic surgery, and in his own production of *In a Lonely Place* (1950), he joked about his appearance. Responding to Gloria Grahame's suggestion that he has an interesting face he looks in the mirror, remarking, 'How could anybody like a face like this?', to which Grahame replies: 'I said I liked it, I didn't say I wanted to kiss it.' Ingrid Bergman had to vouch for Bogart's sex appeal to a dubious Jack Warner before he was definitely assigned to *Casablanca* (1942).

In the film that started him off on leading roles in major films and the attendant romantic opportunities, *The Maltese Falcon* (1941), he apparently dispensed with all make-up, and he was prepared to look his worst if it suited the part. In one startling moment in *The Treasure of the Sierra Madre* (1948), his dusty hobo rises from the chair of a Tampico barber's shop looking like a cleaned-up cadaver with his remaining real hair slicked down and his bony forehead jutting out. Equally bold and devastating was the filthy ruin he allowed himself to become in *The African Queen* (1952), with his stained shirt, stubbled chin and unruly stomach.

Bogart did however have his vain side. If the part didn't require otherwise, he liked to dress smartly in later years and nearly always sported a bow-tie from *Tokyo Joe* (1949) onwards, while in that most appearance-conscious of films, *Beat the Devil* (1953), he is shown selecting and fastening his neckwear. Though he allowed himself to be photographed off set with thinning hair in the mid-1940s, he subsequently vetoed shots in which his hairpiece was not in place.

But Bogart appreciated the value of a distinctive face and there must have been times when the conventional good-lookers like Robert Taylor and Alan Ladd gazed at him in envy.

Bogart's voice, with its slight lisp, was also unusual. Coarse in *The Petrified Forest*, and other early roles where his dialogue was of the 'dis', 'dat' and 'dose' variety, he was never comfortable donning an accent (though off-screen Bogart was reputedly a brilliant mimic of fellow players, like Sydney Greenstreet). But as he proved in *The Maltese Falcon*, the speech impediment was no impediment at all: when tearing into the District Attorney, Bogart spoke cleanly, fast, forcefully, at a dizzy pace, pausing considerately to enquire whether the stenographer was keeping up.

Bogart was also one of the great performers with a cigarette. It gave his hands a prop to work with. He would hang it distinctively from the right hand corner of his mouth before lighting it up. As he emerges from a drab apartment block in *The Harder They Fall* (1956), he pauses to light one before striding forward and thereby emphasizes his first appearance in the film. In *The Big Sleep* (1946), he makes a phone call from a hamburger joint, pausing to take a light from the girl at the counter, solely to introduce the latest in the long succession of glamorous women he encounters in that film. In *The Maltese Falcon*, Bogart smartly divests Peter Lorre's Joel Cairo of his pointed gun, slaps him onto the sofa (after pausing very briefly for the audience to relish Cairo's imminent come-uppance), and all the while retains a cigarette in his mouth to suggest how little effort it cost him. He humiliates Wilmer (Elisha Cook Jr.), by blowing a stream of cigarette smoke into his face and having him removed from the hotel lobby. In *Casablanca* (1942), the haze of cigarette smoke around his melancholy figure helps to blur the image into the flashback sequence.

Bogart was the antithesis of the deadpan, laconic,

ambling, or hearty kind of screen hero. He was a nervous, hypersensitive figure. His face was like a seismograph recording the release of energy elsewhere and his features would crease up alarmingly with any kind of routine physical exertion like packing a suitcase or reaching down to tie a shoelace. It was only to be expected that his gangsters would behave in a violent, unpredictable way, but even his later roles seemed to retain some of this anger, waiting to be unleashed.

When Bogart exploded, the display was very frightening. In *The Maltese Falcon* he throws a fit of the temper to make an impression on Sydney Green-street's Fat Man and walks out on him. In the corridor outside his room, Bogart grins to himself and glances at his hands which are still shaking from the energy he has poured into his act. Real anger is no different: after he has shot one of the Vichy French in *To Have and Have Not* (1944), he holds the rest at gunpoint and has to transfer his weapon from one hand to the other since he is trembling so much. His look indicates to the surviving villains just how near they came to being shot. In *The Big Sleep* (1946), Bogart confronts Eddie Mars (John Ridgely), and terrifies the cold-blooded killer into being blasted to death by his own men, in the ambush he planned to spring on Bogart. The urgency in Bogart's voice, the shots he fires at Eddie, are convincing reasons for Eddie to take his chances outside. Bogart's heavy breathing as he telephones the police indicates how much nervous energy he has put into the confrontation, knowingly placing himself in Eddie's trap with only his gun and the advantage of surprise to extricate himself.

During *In a Lonely Place* (1950), only the twitch in his right cheek betrays his rising anger with the man who is teasing a friend, before he turns and punches the bully to the floor. Here the violence is all the more disturbing, coming from a man of intelligence; a writer by profession. In the same film, the way Bogart's hands shake as he tries to light a cigarette is an alarming expression of his agitation when he realises he is being betrayed by the woman he loves.

Even his smaller gestures could enhance a film. Bogart's 'involuntary' grimace aimed at his former mistress (Gladys George) when her back is turned always delights audiences watching *The Maltese Falcon*. Then there is the moment in *In a Lonely Place* when two old ladies interrupt his conversation in a restaurant, and Bogart nods to himself with faint amusement: another touch that colours a part, making the Bogart character more real and convincingly human.

But it was not only the incidental or sharp reaction – like his tight-lipped disgust with his partner James Cagney's high-handed behaviour in *The Roaring Twenties* (1939) – that Bogart conveyed. There was also the deep-seated feeling that leads him, masochistically, to revive old emotional torments in *Casablanca*.

Bogart's actions and reactions were usually carefully considered; only under extreme circumstances did he act with abandon. One of the more atypical but extraordinary and appealing moments in his entire career occurs in *The African Queen*: after the frail vessel has survived a barrage of German bullets and a hazardous descent through rapids, Bogart tosses away Katharine Hepburn's hat and seizes her for a jubilant kiss. But so expansive a gesture is frowned upon by many Bogart admirers, who find it too extravagant and therefore demeaning.

Bogart was skilled in the art of listening. Bogart knew how to ensure that you noticed he was listening as much as you noticed what other players were saying. In *The Big Sleep*, he practised fingering his right ear lobe thoughtfully – an understandable response to the daunting complexities of the plot – and this was a device among many, seen in other films without the same emphasis or frequency of use. He was employing this mannerism as early as *China Clipper* (1936), and as late as *The Left Hand of God* (1955). In *China Clipper*, he and Ross Alexander are on equal pegging as characters and have separate close-ups seated in a classroom. Ross Alexander just listens to teacher; Bogart listens and toys with his ear. In *The Maltese Falcon*, Bogart sits beside Mary Astor taking in her lies of the day. His finger thoughtfully brushes his lower lip. At other times, in this and other pictures throughout his career, Bogart would stroke his forehead, pinch his nose, rub his chin and do all manner of physical tricks that seem spontaneous but were deliberate. It would be wrong to exaggerate this aspect of Bogart's craft, or to suggest that other actors didn't practise the same or similar devices, but they were part of Bogart's particular alertness and depth as a performer, lending substance to his basic screen magnetism.

'I have heard people say he wasn't *really* a good actor. I don't go along with that,' wrote Mary Astor in her autobiography, *A Life on Film*. 'It is true his personality dominated the character he was playing – but the character gained by it. His technical skill was quite brilliant. His precision timing was no accident. He kept other actors on their toes because he *listened* to them, he watched, he *looked* at them. He never had that vague stare of a person who waited for you to finish talking, who hasn't heard a word you have said. And he was never 'upstage centre' acting all by himself. He was there. With you.'

It is a view confirmed by Van Johnson, who starred with him years later in *The Caine Mutiny*. 'He was one of the most thorough actors I ever knew. Unlike most stars, he would remain in a scene acting his part even though the cameras were trained on someone else. This was undoubtedly the result of his highly professional stage training and experience.'

'He was a complete professional,' remarked writer-director Delmer Daves. 'There was never a day you came to work that he wasn't prepared and ready. Even if he had been drinking as he sometimes did far into the night, it didn't seem to interfere at all with either his memory or his brilliance as an actor. He was good.'

Even the studio boss that Bogart liked to call a 'creep', Jack L. Warner, could recall only one instance of finding his ornery star drunk. In his autobiography *My First Hundred Years in Hollywood*, Warner describes Bogart, wearing dirty pyjamas, riding a bicycle unsteadily around the lot, when he should have been working. Warner remembered berating Bogart over the risk of a fall damaging his face and the threat his conduct posed to the livelihood of the others on the picture. Bogart promised it would never happen again, and Warner reports that it never did.

This conduct came in one period of particular emotional stress, and Howard Hawks claimed to have had to straighten Bogart out in a similar way: 'His taste for Scotch was famous: one day when we'd just started *To Have and Have Not*, he got back from lunch unsteady on his feet. I said to him, "Bogie, you're not that good an actor that you can cope when you've got a few drinks in you." "Too bad," he said, "I like my drink." "Right," I said, "then either I need a new actor, or you need a new director." He never drank at lunch again.' To Hawks, '... he was an extremely hard-working actor. He'd always pretend that he wasn't, that he didn't give a damn, but that wasn't true.'

'The only thing an actor owes his public is a good performance', Bogart liked to say. And that he always delivered. He was proud of his craft. He had acquired his mastery of technique the hard way, through years of practice on the stage. Yet he quickly grasped the essential truth of performing for the movie camera – to underplay, to let the audience do the work by reading emotion through the eyes and the slightest changes of expression. He could learn his lines fast (if necessary, while being made-up for the camera early in the morning), and he was never unprepared. His range may have been narrow – though his work in *The Treasure of the Sierra Madre* and *The African Queen* showed it could be extended successfully beyond urban types – but within his field he was the best.

2

FROM BABY FOOD TO BROADWAY

When a person has been a Hollywood legend, biographical details become suspect. A celebrity could not have a dull history, as the press needed colourful details to interest the public. The performers themselves realised this and were happy to embroider their past with phoney incidents or allow the studio publicists to do it for them. In a 1942 sketch of Bogart, the serious reference publication *Current Biography* was understandably cautious about Bogart's hobbies and interests: 'It is reported that he likes to sketch and paint, to play the bull fiddle, and to make chessmen out of ivory. It is reported, too, that his favourite flower is the hibiscus.'

Bogart confessed in 1953: 'In my younger and wilder days in Hollywood, when I got bored, I used to sit around with one or two of the columnists, and help cook up stories. I liked to see how far I could go and still get the story printed. Someone dug out a cutting the other day that says I had a secret yearning to play the bull fiddle in the orchestra. That, as a matter of fact, I was an expert at it. Take it from me, that's all bull without the fiddle. I probably thought up the story myself, though. Just as I invented the one about Paul Muni, that he had a secret beard room where he kept all his beards. And that one day the wind had swept them all away. A nice touch that, I think. Sure, the yarn was printed. I've told you before, those boys will print

11

anything.' In fact, Bogart was an accomplished chess player and a passionate sailor, but his main hobby was sitting around drinking and talking.

At least Bogart was able to keep his first name. 'Humphrey' was fine for a character actor or villain and it was too late for Hollywood to do anything about it when he became a romantic idol.

He was born Humphrey DeForest Bogart in New York City.

The young Humphrey's date of birth is contentious. Biographical data on Bogart before he caught on in Hollywood gives his birthdate as 23 January 1899. But when Bogart became a studio contract player at Warner Bros. after *The Petrified Forest*, a change took place. The industry reference book *Motion Picture Almanac* lists his birthdate as 23 January 1899 until its 1937–38 edition when it is changed to 25 December 1900. And it is this more colourful date that persists, and that Bogart himself then quoted and lived by (although he modified the year to 1899).

It made an interesting publicity angle. Not only was he 'a Christmas present to his parents', but he could beef to the press that he was always being done out of birthday presents by arriving on Christmas Day. During his marriage to Lauren Bacall, he adhered to this date and they gave annual Christmas Eve parties to celebrate it. She was quite emphatic in her 1988 television tribute, *Bacall on Bogart*: 'Despite what you may have heard or read, Bogie *was* born on Christmas Day 1899 ...'

Humphrey started life not in some hell's kitchen but with a silver spoon in his mouth. His parents were affluent figures, prominent on the social register. They lived in a large brownstone house at 245, West 103rd Street in Manhattan, near the Hudson river. His father, Belmont DeForest Bogart, was a physician in general practice in a fashionable area. His mother,

12

Maud Humphrey Bogart, was a popular and prosperous commercial artist, known by her maiden name of Humphrey. Her illustrations appeared in children's books, magazines and advertisements. The family had a country place on Lake Canandaigua, one of the Finger Lakes of upstate New York. The infant Bogart was largely cared for by the servants (four in all, mostly Irish). His mother's career ate into the time she had for her son and two daughters – Frances, born in 1901, and Kay, born in 1903 – and Bogart would later declare that he had respected rather than loved his mother. When she sketched Humphrey as an infant, she sold the portrait to Mellins, a leading manufacturer of baby foods. Thus Bogart became famous for the first time as 'the Maud Humphrey baby' whose sweet and jolly features smiled at readers from advertisements in all the women's magazines and from the label of the product itself.

It was not a happy childhood for him or for his sisters. He later recalled his parents' rows: 'We kids would pull the covers over our ears to keep out the sound of fighting. Yet that home was kept together – for our sakes and for marriage's sake. And they became adjusted, too, and stopped quarrelling long before we were grown.'

Humphrey was taken on trips by his father – they often went sailing on Lake Canandaigua, and he developed his life-long passion for the water. In 1909, he was enrolled at the strictly-run Trinity School in New York City where he was an undistinguished pupil. When home, he and playmate Bill Brady, son of theatre impresario William A. Brady, used to be given seats in a box for matinees at Brady's Playhouse Theatre. Bogart later claimed that they behaved disgracefully and heckled H.B. Warner during a performance.

One of Brady's directors, John Cromwell, later recalled: 'I put Humphrey Bogart on the stage when he was a kid: he used to hang around the Playhouse Theatre with young Bill Brady and another kid named 'Bull' Durham. They sat in on rehearsals just from interest, and a situation came up with one of those comedies where a part is underwritten and you can't get a good boy to do it so you compromise. That's what this was. Somebody thought of Bogart, who at the time was the most responsible, the most charming ... the best of the three kids. He was, of course, goggle-eyed to do it, and I think he said to me once, "Mr. Cromwell, what do I do? Do I face out to the audience when I speak my lines, or do I talk to the characters?" I went through all these things with him, but the play was an awful flop.'

In September 1917 Humphrey went off to attend his father's *Alma Mater*, Phillips Academy in Andover, Massachusetts. In May 1918 he was expelled for failing to achieve a proper academic standard, though he and studio publicists later maintained it was for pranks like staying out late. By this time his father was in financial difficulties as the result of bad investments, and Humphrey decided to join the Navy in June rather than go home.

He spent two years as a seaman, mainly criss-crossing the Atlantic on the huge troop carriers *U.S.S. Leviathan* and *Santa Olivia*. During that time he damaged the right side of his upper lip. But how? The usual explanation is that it occurred during a U-boat attack. Here's a quote attributed to Bogart in a July 1937 *Photoplay* piece: 'Submarines? A big thrill. Now I tremble when I think of those death dealing machines sticking their noses up over the water. Shells? Why, it was all part of the fun when one hit the side of the boat and splintered it. A piece of wood lodged in my lip. That's where I got this scar.' In fact, the war was over by the time Bogart had finished training, and biographer Richard Gehman was told by Bogart's brother-in-law that he was wounded when, escorting a

14

prisoner between naval bases, the man hit him in the face with his handcuffs, causing Bogart to shoot and injure his prisoner in self-defence.

Honourably discharged from the Navy in 1919, Bogart seems to have tried routine desk jobs: among those mentioned are work for a shipping company, freight-checking for the railroad, and being a runner for Wall Street brokers. Then Bogart got a job through his old pal, Bill Brady Jr., whose father had formed World Films and entered movie production at the Fort Lee, New Jersey studios. During shooting of a Nita Naldi production, *Life*, the impresario quarrelled with his director, Travers Vale, and supposedly sat the office boy, young Bogart, in the director's chair with orders to finish the picture. Not unexpectedly, he floundered, and Brady himself is said to have taken over.

Next we find Bogart as company manager on tours of Brady's stage productions, work which also entailed understudying the male parts and playing minor roles. One such part was that of a Japanese houseboy: he walked on stage with a tray of cocktails and uttered a single line and dropped his tray. In 1920, while on tour with *The 'Ruined' Lady*, starring Brady's actress wife Grace George, he took over the role of a young juvenile drunk, Bill Bruce, from Neil Hamilton for the last matinee of the tour at Newark, New Jersey.

It was during this period that Bogart met his first wife, Helen Menken. She was slightly younger than him, an actress from childhood who became a leading Broadway star thanks to her success in *Seventh Heaven* (1922).

As Bogart related in the British fan magazine *Picturegoer* (18 April 1953): 'I was stage managing a pretty complicated show with a lot of scene changes. Helen was the star. Instead of staying in her dressing-room while these were going on and keeping out of the way, she hung around, slowing things up. I told her to get back to her room. She pulled the great star act on me. I lost my temper. I guess I shouldn't have done it, but I booted her. What more logical than that she should very shortly become the first Mrs. Humphrey Bogart? You'll read in some of the fiction that's been put out about me that my marriage to Helen lasted a month. That's not so. It lasted a year. Mind you, we were together only a month. That, probably, was the trouble. She had to go her way in shows, I had to go mine. How can you keep a marriage together when neither of you ever sees the other? We agreed to call it a day.'

Helen had been doubtful from the first. 'Helen didn't want to marry me because she was wise enough to know about theatrical homes where husbands and wives are continually separated,' he recalled in his 1937 *Photoplay* interview. Although they took out a marriage licence in 1922, they didn't get legally hitched until 20 May 1926, by which time he had become well established as an actor.

He made his first recorded Broadway appearance, billed as Humphrey D. Bogart, with two minor speaking roles in William A. Brady's production of *Drifting*, which opened on 2 January 1922 for a run of sixty-three performances. The melodrama, set in China, starred Brady's daughter, Alice, and Robert Warwick. Bogart played the third husband and a Chinese coolie. It was directed by John Cromwell.

His second Broadway appearance that year was as the juvenile lead, a young romeo called Tom Proctor, with some seventy lines to speak, in another William A. Brady production called *Swifty*, again directed by John Cromwell. In the *New York Herald* (17 October 1922), he was impaled on the vitriolic pen of critic Alexander Woollcott, who concluded his notice of the comedy by writing: '… the young man who embodies the aforesaid sprig is what is usually and mercifully described as inadequate.' Bogart claimed he was so scared on opening night, he walked off stage in the middle of a scene to get a drink of water, temporarily leaving the other actors high and dry. He never disputed Woollcott's verdict and loved to quote the review in later years when he could laugh it off.

He sought easier work in the movies and was one of many actors who tested for the male lead in *The White Sister*, but Ronald Colman won the part which launched him on his illustrious American screen career. Bogart ventured on Broadway again in 1923 in *Meet the Wife*, which opened on 26 November. The comedy by Lynn Starling was a hit and ran for 261 performances. Its star was Mary Boland, while Clifton Webb and Bogart (as a reporter, Gregory Brown) were the juveniles and became life-long friends. After seeing Bogart's performance in *Meet the Wife* Alexander Woollcott generously retracted his earlier remarks: 'Mr. Bogart is a young actor whose last appearance was recorded by your correspondent in words so disparaging that it is surprising to find him still acting. Those words are hereby eaten.'

If, as legend has it, Bogart was the first to say 'Tennis, anyone?' it was in this play. He was to become dreadfully familiar with juvenile leads and defined them as characters who kept the play going while the principals nipped off stage to change their costumes.

In 1924, William A. Brady Jr. turned stage director and recruited Bogart for a small but important role in a ponderous war drama, *Nerves*, that opened on 1 September and died after sixteen performances. Bogart played Bob Thatch, the brother of the heroine (Winifred Lenihan), who is loved by two flying daredevils. Also in the cast was a young actress named Mary Philips, who found Bogart very polite, upright and well-spoken.

The distinguished actress Louise Brooks has also recalled the Bogart of that year. 'In 1924, my first impression of Humphrey Bogart was of a slim boy with charming manners, who was unusually quiet for an actor. His handsome face was made extraordinary by a most beautiful mouth. It was very full, rosy, and perfectly modelled – perfectly, that is, except that, to make it completely fascinating, at one corner of his upper lip a scarred, quilted piece hung down in a tiny scallop. When Humphrey went into films, a surgeon sewed up the scallop, and only a small scar remained. Photographically, it was an improvement, but I missed this endearing disfigurement.'

Early in 1925 Bogart gained another juvenile lead, as Jimmy Todhunter, romancing Shirley Booth in her stage debut, in a comedy called *Hell's Bells* that enjoyed a healthy Broadway run of 139 performances. Then, on 7 September, came the Broadway opening of what proved to be the comedy smash hit of the year, *Cradle Snatchers*. Mary Boland, Edna May Oliver and Margaret Dale were three neglected and not-so-young wives who hired three young collegians to romance them and arouse their husbands' jealousy. According to theatre historian Edwin Bronner, 'Bogart was the most amorous of the three youths, a hot-blooded Latin charmer named José Vallejo. He wowed the ladies.'

In 1937, the actor himself recalled: 'When I was on the road in *Cradle Snatchers* playing the role of the Spanish osteopath, all the old women in the audience thought because I played such a part I must be such a guy. I wish I'd saved the notes that came to the theatre. They would make you sick.' He also had a more welcome admirer in a prominent lady critic, Amy Leslie, who reviewed the Chicago try-out and remarked: 'Humphrey Bogart created a furor ... He is as young and handsome as Valentino, as dexterous and elegant in comedy as E.H. Sothern, as graceful as any of our best romantic actors.' *Cradle Snatchers* ran for 485 performances in New York, was made into a silent movie by Howard Hawks in 1927, and was later transformed into the 1943 Bob Hope comedy, *Let's Face It*.

It was during this play's run that Bogart felt confident enough to marry Helen Menken and after it that his career nose-dived. Roscoe 'Fatty' Arbuckle made a doomed attempt to retrieve some of his pre-scandal popularity by starring in a revival of a 1910 comedy hit, *Baby Mine*. Lee Patrick played the wife who pretends to be a mother, Bogart was Alfred Hardy, the businessman husband she wants to win back, and Arbuckle played the wife's friend who finds a real baby to aid her deception. It opened on 9 June 1927 to first night applause described by *The New York Times* as 'of almost record length', but the mass of theatre-goers stayed away and it collapsed after twelve performances. Bogart went in search of work to Chicago, while Helen starred in the London West End production of *Seventh Heaven*. Soon their marriage was in trouble.

Later in the year, Bogart joined the cast of the hit comedy *Saturday's Children* by Maxwell Anderson. Directed by Guthrie McClintic, it was a drama of a hard-pressed working-class marriage which starred Ruth Gordon as the wife, and which had opened with Roger Pryor as the husband, Rims O'Neil. Bogart took over from Pryor during the run of 310 performances. One of the play's three film versions, released by Warner Bros. in 1940, with John Garfield and Anne Shirley, is well remembered.

Bogart was now hitting it off with Mary Philips and arranged a divorce from Helen Menken (they were to remain on cordial terms for the rest of his life; she remarried twice and died in 1966). Bogart and Mary Philips were married during April 1928. Later that year, Bogart obtained what was probably his first film work, supporting Helen Hayes in a two-reeler called *The Dancing Town*, written by Rupert Hughes. This was made in New York as the third in a Paramount series called 'Great Stars and Authors', a hangover from the studio's 'Famous Players in Famous Plays' days.

19

Whereas Bogart's first marriage had been unbalanced by his wife's greater standing professionally, he and Mary had achieved the same level of moderate success in their acting careers. Happily, Guthrie McClintic cast them as husband and wife in the lead roles of his next production, a comedy drama called *Skyrocket*, but unhappily it survived for a mere eleven performances after opening on 11 January 1929. Written by Mark Reed, it presented Bogart as an ambitious inventor, Vic Ewing, whose temporary success leads him to overlook his devoted wife and father.

Still, its failure meant that Bogart was available to take over on a few hours' notice from Guido Nazo as the male lead in the current William A. Brady production starring Brady's sister Alice, *A Most Immoral Lady*. This comedy by Townsend Martin, about a woman blackmailer who reforms, came off in April 1929 after 160 performances.

Bogart had good fortune appearing in the comedy *It's a Wise Child* which made its debut on 6 August 1929 and survived the Wall Street crash in October to rack up 378 performances. Mildred McCoy played a single girl, engaged to an older man (Harlan Briggs), who feigns pregnancy so that she can break it off and take up with Humphrey Bogart's young Roger Baldwin, (it became a 1931 Marion Davies movie).

The success of talking pictures gave an advantage to Broadway actors who had proved they knew how to speak clearly. Many of them were used by Warner Bros. as supporting players in a long series of talking shorts starring leading vaudeville artistes and made by a Warner subsidiary, the Vitaphone Corporation, in Brooklyn. So it was that Humphrey Bogart supported singer Ruth Etting in a one-reeler, *Broadway's Like That*, released in March 1930. It offered 'The star of *Whoopee* in a dramatic playlet with two songs', and all in eight minutes. She portrayed a girl from the sticks and

Bogart was her companion in a lunchtime scene at a Chinese restaurant. The film image of this short survives but the sound (on a separate disc) has been mislaid. In a *Film Fan Monthly* article (September 1974), based on an interview with Ruth Etting, W. Franklyn Moshier noted, 'Ruth recalled that Bogart tried giving her acting pointers for this venture. He was very patient and went over the lines with her, making suggestions as to how they might be delivered. The critics felt the singing portion outshone her abilities to read lines convincingly.'

For actors like Bogart this kind of film work was just a useful sideline. It wasn't an alternative career to the stage. To be in the movies you had to go to Hollywood.

3

TO HOLLYWOOD AND BACK

The Fox company was one of the Hollywood studios looking for well-spoken Broadway players who might fit into the new era of talking pictures. With a brother-in-law working in Fox's New York office, Bogart was soon screen-tested. The results were encouraging enough to put him on a westbound train with the promise of starring in a remake of the 1924 hit, *The Man Who Came Back*. But the same carrot had been dangled in front of other hopefuls from the East and the role was eventually assigned to an established movie star, Charles Farrell. Bogart was given the consolatory position of voice coach on the production. His wife Mary had stayed in New York to continue appearing in a play. Fox were clearly serious about using Bogart and gave him good roles in two of their big 1930 releases.

Since he had made his reputation in light comedy, it is no surprise to discover that he was handed parts in like vein. *Up the River* gave Bogart the chance to work with John Ford, even then a front-rank director, though he reputedly made a poor impression on Ford by being too familiar and calling him Jack. He was never to work with the director again. (Another young Fox hopeful of that time, John Wayne, treated Ford with more deference and was eventually given the starring role in *Stagecoach*.) A broad comedy, *Up the River* was about a couple of tough convicts, St. Louis (Spencer Tracy in his feature debut) and his thickheaded pal, Dannemora Dan (Warren Hymer). The pair befriend Bogart's Steve, who is serving time for 'accidental manslaughter'. Bogart falls in love with a girl in the women's wing who was the dupe of a swindler. When he gets out and returns home to his parents (who think he's been abroad), a blackmailer threatens to expose his past. The two convicts escape from jail and sort out his troubles, enabling him to marry the girl (Claire Luce) and live happily ever after. Then the pair return to prison for an important baseball game.

The story has striking similarities to one of Bogart's favourite later films, *We're No Angels* (1955). 'Efficient' was the word *The New York Times* attached to Bogart's work in *Up the River*. According to William K. Everson, who has viewed the one badly damaged print that survives, 'Bogart is amusingly subdued in the scenes where as an ex-convict now living with a mother unaware of his past, he dutifully calls "Coming, mother!", and trots downstairs like a slightly cynical Henry Aldrich!'

A Devil with Women partnered him with burly Victor McLaglen, who had a role little removed from his famous Captain Flagg characterisation – a mercenary seeking to capture a revolutionary in a banana republic. Bogart was a sort of junior Quirt as Tom Standish, McLaglen's ally and romantic rival who is eventually successful in both winning the girl (Mona Maris) and keeping the older man's friendship. Said Mordaunt Hall in *The New York Times*: '... there is an irritating friend with his trick of getting the last laugh, whether it be at martial or at amorous adventure. The last is Humphrey Bogart who ... gives an ingratiating performance. Mr. Bogart is both good-looking and intelligent.' Yet by modern standards he now appears to have been trying too hard – not a criticism applicable to his later work.

Suddenly Fox seemed to lose interest in him.

Someone must have decided he would never make the grade. In the 1931 release *Body and Soul*, he portrayed Jim Watson, an American flyer in an R.A.F. squadron in France during World War I. Although he has an American wife, he has become involved with a girl in England. He dies trying to bring down a German observation balloon, leaving his pal (played by Charles Farrell) to complete the job and award him credit posthumously. Most of the picture detailed Farrell's adventures with Bogart's widow and his English girlfriend, one of whom turns out to be a German spy.

During the making of the film, Bogart spent two weeks wedged in a cockpit with Farrell for night flying scenes and apparently tried to make the most of his limited screen time by edging himself into the centre of the frame and generally upsetting his co-star to the extent that, if a 1938 *Photoplay* article is to be believed, they almost came to blows. Farrell had a boat and weekends spent sailing brought them together even if they weren't always on speaking terms at the outset.

Fox dispatched Bogart to Universal for another 1931 release, *Bad Sister*. He played a heel called Valentine Corliss who romances the daughter (Sidney Fox), of a wealthy businessman and uses her to extract money from wealthy townspeople for a mythical factory scheme. He decamps with the girl, abandoning her at the first opportunity, leaving her to return home sadder and wiser. Bette Davis made her screen debut as the foolish girl's younger sister. Carl Laemmle Jr., the new head of production at Universal, is said to have advised both Davis and Bogart that they didn't photograph well and should hasten back to the stage. Viewed today, the picture shows Bogart giving an assured performance but Davis failing lamentably.

Bogart's fortunes declined even further at Fox when he reported for *Women of All Nations*. He was no longer sharing the action with star Victor McLaglen as he had in *A Devil with Women* but was cast as one of the supporting gang, a marine called Stone, in this second sequel to *What Price Glory?* Even more humiliating than coming ninth in the published cast, however, was his total absence from the film after it lost half an hour of footage just before its release in mid-1931. A surviving print, at the full, though rather brief, running time, shows no sign of him or several other billed players, including Joyce Compton and Charles Judels, although his appearance is preserved in stills from the film.

Fox rubbed in Bogart's downfall by giving him a role in one of its George O'Brien westerns, *A Holy Terror*. It was a sad fate for a stage actor, not only to be playing in a fifty-three-minute cowboy programmer but being padded out in the shoulders and fitted with elevator shoes to make a more manly impression (Bogart was 5ft 9½ins tall). His part in the modern-day tale was that of ranch foreman Steve Nash and it required him to sulk when a dashing millionaire (O'Brien) flies in from the East and takes away his girl (Sally Eilers).

Next at Fox he was supposed to go into a Spencer Tracy drama called *She Wanted a Millionaire*, but he didn't, unless his part was too small to receive credit when the film made its appearance in 1932. He quit the studio and retraced his steps to Broadway.

He trod the boards once again, sporting a moustache, in John van Druten's comedy-drama *After All*, appearing as Duff Wilson, boyfriend of the heroine (Margaret Perry). Playing an oppressive matriarch, the British actress Helen Haye was the principal star, but the production died after a mere twenty performances in December 1931.

By this time, the Depression had begun to hurt Bogart. The family fortune had gone, his father was barely working and only his mother was bringing in money with her drawing. It was some relief to be summoned back to Hollywood by Harry Cohn, head of Columbia Pictures, for the top male role in *Love Affair*

(1932). The film was essentially a vehicle for an English actress, Dorothy Mackaill, a silent star struggling to keep a career in talkies. Columbia was not then a major studio – it made a habit of picking up other studios' discards (John Wayne also went there after Fox was through with him). But the part was a meaty one. Mackaill is an heiress; Bogart is Jim Leonard, an engineer trying to promote a new aircraft engine. They have an affair but she breaks it up rather than distract him from his work. She even agrees to marry another suitor in order to finance Bogart's engine. Following various plot complications, she is only saved from committing suicide by his last minute arrival. While the part did not revitalise Bogart's screen career, it enabled him to strike up a friendship with Harry Cohn, to be revived years later when Bogart went into production for himself.

The actor is usually associated with Warner Bros. in film histories, and rightly so, for he made far more pictures there than anywhere else. The Ruth Etting short had been produced by a Warner subsidiary, and he played in his first Warner features in Hollywood during 1932, but his roles were little more than bits.

Big City Blues is a minor comedy-drama about a callow youth from Indiana (Eric Linden), who spends three hectic days in the big city of New York being fleeced by a cousin and suspected of murder. Bogart appears as Shep Adkins, by profession an assistant theatre treasurer, who is a member of the drinking party that assembles in the boy's hotel room. He quarrels over a woman with another guest (Lyle Talbot), and they start to fight, making use of broken bottles. The fight spreads, the room is plunged into darkness, and a girl is murdered ... It is interesting now to watch Bogart getting the feel of a touchy, truculent character; the familiar traits are there, but a little stiff and subdued. The part is strictly one-dimensional but the actor gives it some substance.

In *Three on a Match*, Bogart makes his first screen appearance as a tough hoodlum or 'mug' called Harve. He leads a gang who work for a big-time gambler (Edward Arnold). Lyle Talbot plays another gambler in debt to Arnold. When Talbot kidnaps the wife (Ann Dvorak) and son of a wealthy lawyer (Warren William), Bogart and his boys butt in to make sure the ransom is properly collected. Bogart here was rather stiff and monotonously menacing, although there is one striking shot of him from a low angle glowering down at the kidnapped boy after he has dared to speak. But there was nothing here to indicate that he would ever make a notable screen villain.

Once again Bogart went back to Broadway where he found more substantial parts. But the going was tough even there; as the Depression bit harder, spending money dried up and few plays lasted a month, though flops often lingered for a while longer than business justified in the hope of attracting a movie sale. Bogart appeared as Randall Williams, an architect, in the romantic comedy drama *I Loved You Wednesday*. He is tempted to leave his wealthy wife (Rose Hobart) for a old flame (Frances Fuller) from his student days in Paris. Henry Fonda had a speechless minor role as a customer in a bar in this modestly successful production (sixty-three performances from October to November, 1932). Fox gave no thought to its former contract artist in casting the 1933 screen version and opted for Warner Baxter as the husband.

Bogart went straight into a melodrama called *Chrysalis* in mid-November, playing Don Ellis, the reckless lover of Margaret Sullavan's spoiled debutante, with June Walker, Elisha Cook Jr., Osgood Perkins and Elia Kazan in supporting roles. This hung on long enough – for twenty-three performances – to be taken up by Hollywood, and Paramount's film version, *All of Me* (1934), went to Fredric March and Miriam Hopkins.

Then there was a comedy called *Our Wife*, which opened on 2 March 1933. Conditions had become so grim that President Roosevelt declared a four-day bank holiday to take some of the pressure off the bankers, which stopped the withdrawal of cash and in the process hit cinema and theatre admissions badly. Bogart was to recall: '*Our Wife* opened the night of the day the banks closed. There were ten people in the house. Things kept on being like that. I thought my career was over. I thought I'd never have any money again.' For the play's twenty performances, Bogart was seen as an errant husband, Jerry Marvin, who runs off to Europe with Rose Hobart only to be chased by his possessive wife, played by June Walker. This also reached the screen, but not until 1941 with Melvyn Douglas, Ruth Hussey and Ellen Drew.

This was followed in May by a Theatre Guild production of *The Mask and the Face*, W. Somerset Maugham's version of an Italian comedy by Luigi Chiarelli, which was limited to a five-week, forty-performance run to complete a subscription series. Judith Anderson starred as an unfaithful wife while Stanley Ridges was the jealous husband who sends her abroad and pretends he has killed her. Bogart had the minor part of Luciano Spina. Shirley Booth, Leo G. Carroll and Ernest Cossart were more prominent supporting players now remembered for later screen work.

Bogart and his wife Mary found work together in summer stock that year at Cohasset, Massachusetts, but it was more than a year before another Broadway production beckoned him. He did receive a welcome call from a stage producer, Chester Erskine: 'We lived near each other at that time in New York. Bogart was a very good actor and still playing juveniles – as he used to describe them, the "Tennis, anyone?" roles. I said, "I'm going to make a film. There's a part in it for you but it's a heavy, a tough guy." And he said, "Well, I can do that!" And he did it – very well. He was intrigued by the thought that he was breaking with his past, he loved the idea of playing a part in which he was not sympathetic. Only a year or so later, he said, "I've talked them into letting me play *The Petrified Forest*," and that was that, he was really off.'

Erskine's film was an independent production called *Midnight* (1934), and he reopened the old Thomas Edison studios where he shot it for less than $50,000. The result was a somewhat pretentious, ironic melodrama. A jury foreman (O.P. Heggie) has been instrumental in dispatching a woman to the electric chair for a crime of passion; at the same instant as the switch is pulled, history repeats itself and his daughter (Sidney Fox), shoots her lover (played by Bogart), in circumstances which mirror the earlier crime; her intention is not to kill him but to stop him going away. As Gus Garboni, Bogart was required to be conventionally handsome in a saturnine way. Appearing only at the beginning and the end, he received a lowly billing in eighth place: very much a supporting player. Caught up in the rackets and headed for Chicago, his Garboni tries to leave the girl behind as he doesn't want her life spoilt, and so his part is not an unsympathetic one. A district attorney takes pity on the girl and passes off the death as a gangland killing. Thanks to Bogart's later success, this film gained a new lease of life in 1947, being reissued in the United States by a skid-row distributor as *Call It Murder* with Bogart misleadingly promoted to star billing.

Certainly, Bogart's stage work was taking him further away from romantic comedy and more towards dramatic roles. *Invitation to a Murder* opened in May 1934, very late in the season, and ran for fifty-two performances. Gale Sondergaard starred in this haunted house thriller as the wealthy matriarch who survives an attempt to poison her and hatches a cunning plan to expose the perpetrator. Suspicion falls on two cousins, but Horatio Channing, the one played by Bogart, proves to be the innocent one. When Warner Bros. turned it into a 1942 B-movie called *The Hidden Hand*, Bogart had thankfully progressed beyond replaying the role.

In September 1934, Bogart's father died, leaving $10,000 in debts and rather more than that in uncollected fees. Bogart was very depressed and according to some reminiscences, practically suicidal.

4

ENTER DUKE MANTEE

While Bogart was appearing in *Invitation to a Murder*, he was noticed by producer Arthur Hopkins who was in the throes of casting *The Petrified Forest*. It seems to have been something about Bogart's voice that suggested him for the role of Duke Mantee, an escaped killer modelled on Dillinger, although the playwright, Robert Emmet Sherwood, thought Bogart best suited to play the footballer, his play's nearest equivalent to a 'Tennis, anyone?' part. Hopkins arranged for Bogart to audition for Mantee, and the play's star, English actor Leslie Howard, had only to hear Bogart to insist on having him. The play tried out in Hartford, Connecticut, then opened in Boston on Christmas Eve 1934 to great acclaim, and arrived in New York on 7 January 1935, settling down for a run of 194 performances.

It began as a really happy New Year for Bogart, but Louise Brooks (in *Lulu in Hollywood*) recalled seeing Bogart a few months later in Tony's Bar on Fifty-Second Street: 'I went in at about one o'clock in the morning and sat at a table near Humphrey, who was sitting in a booth with the actor Thomas Mitchell. It was a few weeks before the Broadway version of *The Petrified Forest* would close in June 1935. Humphrey had nothing to look forward to except summer stock in Skowhegan, Maine. Presently, Mitchell paid his bill and went out, leaving Humphrey alone, drinking steadily, with weary determination. His head drooped lower and lower. When I left, he had fallen into his exhausted sleep, with his head sunk in his arms on the table. "Poor Humphrey," I said to Tony. "He's finally licked." '

The play closed on 29 June – it might have gone on longer, but Leslie Howard wanted a break. Bogart went off to Skowhegan and appeared in such plays as *Rain* and *Ceiling Zero* during August.

The film rights to *The Petrified Forest* had been snapped up by Warner Bros. who were more than pleased to retain Leslie Howard in the screen version. But they didn't want a Hollywood has-been to play Duke Mantee, and certainly not when they had Edward G. Robinson under contract. Fortunately, Robinson was tired of gangster parts and turned this one down while an alarmed Bogart rallied Leslie Howard to his cause. Howard obliged by quietly insisting that he would play with no one but Humphrey Bogart. Warners made several tests before signing him to a standard contract for just the one film, and he reported to the lot in October 1935. His wife Mary was busy playing Roland Young's wife in the play *A Touch of Brimstone* so stayed in New York.

Bogart knew his Duke Mantee inside out by now and the nearly foolproof part had a gloomy aspect that suited his personality better than the flippancy of lighter roles. This time Bogart would succeed in Hollywood.

Seen today, *The Petrified Forest* is something of a creaking curiosity, especially during the Bogartless opening half-hour. It is a very faithful screen adaptation rather than an interpretation, content to stick with material that had been shown to work on the stage. The setting – a remote service station and café in the rugged Arizona desert – is impressively but obviously created on the Warner sound stages, lending a useful 'closed-in' feeling to the film. A friendship blossoms between two sensitive, lonely people: a

32

penniless British wanderer (Leslie Howard), who is seeking to put some meaning back into his life and a French-born waitress (Bette Davis), who yearns to escape from her deadening surroundings. Then Humphrey Bogart's Duke Mantee arrives with his gang of hoods. A killer who, radio broadcasts tell us, has left eight men dead in a shoot-out in Oklahoma City, he takes over the place and awaits the arrival of his girlfriend.

Bogart's performance is powerful and primitive. He shuffles about the café setting, round-shouldered from the weight of his chest-holsters, hands hanging limply in front of him as though in prison chains, head dropping forward and sinking into his shoulders, making it only too clear that he is one of the 'apes' with whom Leslie Howard earlier compared intellectuals like himself, when talking about the future of mankind. Bogart speaks his lines wearily; his slow, clear enunciation would seem to be a leftover from his stage experience in the role. His Mantee is in sharp contrast to the aggressive, volatile, optimistic public enemies of earlier Hollywood films. 'This is Duke Mantee, the world-famous killer, and he's hungry,' says one of his gang as he first enters, reducing the legend to a common-place figure.

'You're the last great apostle of rugged individualism,' declares Leslie Howard, raising his glass in salute to Bogart who has settled down, shotgun resting on his lap, on a platform a step above his prisoners like a king on a throne. Bogart spits out the end he has bitten off a cigar and responds to Howard's tribute – 'Maybe you're right, pal' – his answer indicating his failure to understand Howard's meaning. 'He ain't no gangster, he's a real old-time desperado. Gangsters is foreigners,' Charley Grapewin's Gramps tells us, but when Leslie Howard invites Bogart to build up his legend by describing his colourful life, the outlaw gives a tired reply: 'Wha' d'you tink? I spend most of my time since

I grew up in jail. And it looks like I spend the rest of my life dead.'

Howard is concerned to ennoble Bogart as a suitable instrument for his own demise, for he arranges with him to be shot dead so that the waitress can receive enough money from his life insurance policy to escape to France. She represents hope for the future in a film where the conventional heroic figure, the burly football player, is ridiculed for his shallowness and philistinism. Howard recognises that both he and Bogart have had their day. But Bogart becomes a figure of pathos when he fails to measure up to Howard's estimation of him. Though he agrees to kill Howard, he refuses to do so until forced to when Howard blocks his escape route. And he proves an indecisive leader when pressurised. 'Shut up! Give me time to think!' Bogart cries when he learns his girl has betrayed their whereabouts and his men exhort him to flee. As he steps past the dying Howard, he stops to say, 'Be seeing you soon'. Moments later his capture by the police is relayed to us.

Twenty years later, Bogart attributed his effectiveness to the way he sat there behind a shotgun: 'Nobody could take their eyes off Duke because they were never sure when he was going to shoot up the place,' and joked about his subsequent career as a killer: 'Leslie Howard was my best shot. I got him with one bullet and he died quick. The others were slow bleeders and most of the time they lived long enough to kill me.'

Fortunately for Bogart and many other actors, playwright Sherwood's attempts to write an epitaph for the American gangster were unsuccessful, and they continued to populate the screen. From seeing the rushes of *The Petrified Forest*, Warner Bros. anticipated that he would probably make a new impact as Duke Mantee and in November 1935 he was signed to a standard seven-year contract with options. Bogart insisted on one thing: time off to play Duke Mantee opposite Robert Donat in a London stage production scheduled for April 1936, but Donat produced and starred in another play, *Red Night*, instead, and when *The Petrified Forest* belatedly opened on stage in London on 16 December 1942, Hartley Power played Mantee to Owen Nares' Alan Squier.

For *The Petrified Forest*, Bogart was given fifth billing, billed after the stars, and Genevieve Tobin and Dick Foran. The studio clearly saw Bogart as a useful work-horse rather than a potential big star as he was given supporting roles in major features and allowed leads only in inconsequential B-movies or exploitable films where the subject was the box-office draw and the name of the star didn't matter a great deal. By the end of 1939, he would be seen in no less than twenty-four films, including two loan-outs.

5

MERELY A CONTRACT PLAYER

Louise Brooks declared that no job in the world more closely resembled slavery than a studio contract. And no studio worked its players harder than Warner Bros., preferring to keep them busy in unsuitable or demeaning roles, even bit parts, and send them on personal appearances and promotional tours when not posing for portraits, rather than have them draw their weekly pay for sitting idle. There was more resentment, more suspensions without pay at Warner Bros. than anywhere else. James Cagney, Bette Davis and Olivia de Havilland were leading malcontents, but Bogart was to become just as discontented with his treatment as they were.

At first, he was merely glad to be busy. During 1936, he completed seven films (although only four of them, plus *The Petrified Forest*, were released during the year, and the seven did not appear in their order of production).

In February, he was dispatched to the Bryan Foy unit at Warner Bros. which made the B-movies and specialised in cheap remakes of the studio's old hits. Foy was known as the Keeper of the Bs, and his method was to take strong situations from successful A films and change the settings and titles to fool audiences into accepting them as new pictures. Thus Bogart found himself playing Edward G. Robinson's newspaper editor from a fierce exposé of yellow journalism, *Five Star Final* (1931), but the setting was now a radio station and the film had been retitled *Two Against the World*. It mounted an uncompromising attack on sensational and irresponsible reporting. Bogart played the part of station manager Sherry Scott who reluctantly accepts his boss's scheme to revive a twenty-year-old scandal, resigns after the broadcast has tragic repercussions, and helps the Radio Commission clean up the station's policies. Bogart could not give his part the maturity that Edward G. Robinson had invested in the original but at least it was a total change from Duke Mantee.

In March, his wife Mary was busy starring on Broadway with Richard Barthelmess in *The Postman Always Rings Twice*. It was around this time, according to Louise Brooks, that Bogart began an affair with actress Mayo Methot, a woman three years younger than him. He and Mary had agreed to an open marriage because of their times apart. 'We were too modern,' Bogart reflected ruefully in 1937. 'I was to go out with other girls. She was to see whom she liked. She was fine – not jealous a bit. I said that was great. She was an understanding wife. But I wanted her to be jealous.' Instead, she made Bogart jealous through an intimate friendship with Roland Young.

In March, Bogart was initially scheduled for a supporting role, either as a murderous jewel thief or a playboy, in *Public Enemy's Wife* which starred Pat O'Brien and Margaret Lindsay; but Cesar Romero and Dick Foran played these roles in the finished picture. He had been reassigned to a bigger and better picture: *Bullets or Ballots*. Though he was playing another gangster, called Nick 'Bugs' Fenner, this one was of the slick, urban variety, clean-shaven and neatly dressed, rather than a Neanderthal like Duke Mantee. His 'Bugs' amounted to quite a lethal figure, responsible during the film for knocking off his crime czar boss, a crusading newspaper editor, and the cop who worms his way into the organisation.

As an actor, Bogart proved to be quite a dangerous scene stealer, especially where Barton MacLane is concerned. At the start of the film, Bogart takes MacLane (as his boss, Al Kruger) to a movie theatre to see a crime documentary in which the latter is denounced as a public enemy. While MacLane turns his back to buy tickets, Bogart moves around in his best alert bodyguard manner. Inside, while MacLane sits there stolidly gazing at the screen, Bogart tugs thoughtfully at his lip and later fingers it again; he shakes his head slightly with amusement at what's on the screen; and he glances at MacLane to see his reaction. All this ensures that one watches Bogart rather than MacLane, who was always a dull if competent performer. Bogart even contrived to gain a lighting advantage in a later scene in MacLane's office, standing over a desk lamp that gives a sinister cast to his features while MacLane sits behind the desk, lit more normally. MacLane is billed above Bogart here, but it is easy to see why MacLane slipped to smaller parts and Bogart went on to bigger things.

Bogart's part is the livelier one, anyway, as the figure who stirs up trouble while MacLane tries to keep things quiet and peaceful: Bogart shoots down Henry O'Neill's newsman on his own initiative and later he appears in MacLane's office in a menacing, slightly low-angle shot to announce that he's taking over and fires his gun to prove the point. Bogart's main adversary is Edward G. Robinson, the former cop who once put him in hospital for a week, but who is now a trusted member of the crime organisation. When Bogart has proof that Robinson is still a cop working undercover, he rushes to the man's boarding house and catches him coming down the stairs. They draw their guns and blaze away. Bogart must die and Robinson survive long enough to incriminate the bankers who are behind the organisation, but Bogart finds a way to fix his death in the audience's mind: as Edward G.

Robinson steps over his corpse, Bogart's hand is lodged against a stair, frozen in a farewell wave.

The next film on which Bogart worked, *China Clipper*, was excitingly topical at the time though now it seems an overweight, undistinguished drama. Pat O'Brien was the airline operator who is inspired by Lindbergh's conquest of the Atlantic to create a new plane to attempt a record-breaking run across the Pacific. Bogart and Ross Alexander are his pilot buddies. Alexander was the more personable actor, and so had the humour and romance; Bogart played a former barnstormer and widower, Hap Stuart, and the more sombre of the two. He tears a strip off O'Brien for his callous treatment of his men, knocking him to the ground and leaving; but he returns to pilot the historical flight. The emphasis, though, is less on his contribution than on a montage of newspaper headlines and O'Brien sweating it out by the wireless on the ground.

China Clipper was a main feature but *Isle of Fury* was an hour-long B-movie filmed under the title *Three in Eden*. It gave Bogart the leading role as a late replacement for Ian Hunter and was another of Bryan Foy's rehashes, this time of *The Narrow Corner* (1933). The new edition threw out the subtleties of the original but clung on to all the plot complications. Bogart's Val Stevens (he sported a moustache for the part) is a wanted man who has hidden himself away as the pearl-fishing owner of a South Seas island. He so impresses Donald Woods, the detective on his trail, that the latter allows him to continue enjoying married life with his bride (Margaret Lindsay). Director Frank McDonald was more concerned to make it quickly than to make it well, and he brought it in considerably ahead of its already short schedule.

The studio's continuing low estimate of Bogart's drawing power was indicated by another role in support of Pat O'Brien. *The Great O'Malley* (begun as

The Making of O'Malley) was a thick slice of Irish whimsy, and had the actor cast as John Phillips, the unemployed family man who is going after a good job when an officious cop, O'Malley (Pat O'Brien), stops his car and fines him for having a noisy silencer. Losing the job, the embittered Bogart turns to a life of crime and is arrested for a pawnshop hold-up when the same O'Malley delays his getaway by catching him with that car silencer still not mended. The cop befriends Bogart's crippled daughter, arranges for an operation on her leg, and wins a parole for Bogart. Unaware that his old enemy has become his benefactor, Bogart shoots him at the first opportunity but the understanding cop passes it off as an accident and everything ends happily ever after.

Black Legion was altogether superior. An example of Warner Bros. in its crusading mood, it cast Bogart as an ordinary worker who joins a xenophobic organisation, the Black Legion, as an outlet for the frustration he experiences at work when a studious Pole (Henry Brandon) gains the promotion he covets.

Bogart's Frank Taylor starts out as a likeable family man, proud of his wife and child and planning to improve their lives with the extra income he expects to receive. His reaction to butter on the table – 'What is this? Christmas or something?' – brings home the real deprivation of the period and the frustration it bred.

Sore at losing the promotion, the Bogart character is susceptible to talk of 'the foreign menace' and 'America for Americans'. It is as a result of specific circumstances rather than his natural disposition that he is ripe for membership of the Black Legion: he joins a little hesitantly and balks at the theatrical language of the pledge of allegiance he has to read during the initiation ceremony. But, once a member, his subsequent disintegration is rapid; tucking a gun into his belt, he admires himself in a full-length mirror. He gets his revenge on the Pole, but wrecks his own marriage, loses his job, and ends up killing his best friend (Dick Foran) after drunkenly confiding his membership of the terror organisation. In court, the old Frank Taylor asserts himself, easing his conscience by a full confession.

Regrettably, the script is too schematic and plodding, harping on Bogart's impending promotion to the point that one knows he isn't going to get it. And the film backs away from the hot social issue it has raised by making the leaders of the Black Legion criminal types motivated not by hatred of foreigners but by the lucrative income to be earned from selling guns and cloaks to a gullible public.

However, Bogart confidently handles a wide range of moods: heady optimism, sullen resentment, drunken self-pity, and stricken remorse. He only overplays one scene, in which he begs his friend Foran not to turn him in: Bogart never could humble himself convincingly. At the courtroom climax, his character is deemed too inarticulate to be allowed the job of denouncing the Black Legion and the scripts assigns the job to the ever eloquent Samuel S. Hinds as the judge, leaving Bogart with only a last distressed look at his wife as he is led away to the cells.

This was a proper A-feature that put Bogart back at work with the director of *The Petrified Forest*, Archie Mayo, but Warners knew the film didn't need a top star because its controversial subject matter would be the main selling point. Certainly Bogart was pleased to be in it. Eighteen months later, before he made the big time, he commented, 'I think *Black Legion* got me as near to where I want to go as anything. At least it got me away from the conventional gangster character.'

From *Black Legion* Bogart went straight into *San Quentin*. It was his third outing in support of Pat O'Brien and his first drama behind bars (*Up the River* was a comedy). It was a high-speed affair in which he capably played the role of a man far younger than himself. He is a cocky twenty-five-year-old, Red Kennedy, going inside for the first time after a career of five years in reform school and a year in the county jail that has left him with an ingrained antisocial attitude. As he proudly boasts, 'I kicked a guy in the face once because he was a cop.'

In the prison yard, he's the one who wears the brim of his regulation hat turned furthest back as a gesture of defiance. Later, he wavers between the good influence of the fair-minded new captain of the prison yard (Pat O'Brien), and the adverse influence of a confirmed criminal (Joe Sawyer). When Bogart learns that his precious sister (Ann Sheridan) is dating the captain, he explodes with rage, broods in his bunk, then stages an escape while on the road gang. He shoots O'Brien before discovering that his sister and O'Brien really love each other. In a brave attempt to make amends, Bogart starts back to the prison, is fired on by the police, and staggers along in a skilfully prolonged collapse that is more reminiscent of ballet than acting. He dies in the shadow of the prison gates exhorting his fellow cons to back up their yard captain. Seen today, *San Quentin* is still fun, an archetypal prison movie which has no delusions of social significance.

Bogart ended 1936 at work on *Marked Woman*. Like *Black Legion*, it was derived from actual events. Bette Davis was the star but Bogart had the next best role. For a change, he played an uncomplicated, incorrigibly honest figure, an assistant district attorney called David Graham who is itching to nail vice czar Johnny Vanning (Eduardo Ciannelli). Bogart's character was modelled on Thomas A. Dewey, who had smashed the prostitution racket of Charles 'Lucky' Luciano. His eagerness to trap his man leads him into trusting Bette Davis's clip-joint hostess (the word 'prostitute' was not permissible), but her evidence is discredited by other witnesses as she well knew it would be. 'So long, chump! I'll be seeing you,' she calls as she breezes out of court past Bogart. Later, however, Davis's younger sister (Jane Bryan) becomes entangled with Ciannelli and meets with a fatal accident at his hands. Bogart at first seems to delight in Davis's distress but, once the sister's body is found and she has been scarred by Ciannelli's men to keep her quiet, he knows he can trust her. He brings a case against Ciannelli, and clinches matters with a long, hard-hitting address to the jury. Bogart reputedly overheard technicians betting on how many takes he would need to get the speech right; he wagered he could do it first time, and won.

Unexpectedly, the film's most telling scene is not the conviction of Ciannelli but the aftermath in which Bogart reaps all the acclaim (he is even hailed as the state's future governor), at the expense of Davis and the other girls whose courageous evidence has made his success possible. Bogart expertly captures the awkwardness of the man as he tries to express his admiration and concern, gratitude and maybe affection for Bette Davis but can only utter the lame promise, 'No matter what you do or where you go, we'll meet again.' 'Goodbye, then, I'll be seeing you,' says Davis wistfully, in complete contrast to her earlier brash farewell in court. They go their separate ways: he back to the flashbulbs of the press photographers, she into the night with the other girls. One of those girls was played by Mayo Methot, soon to become Bogart's third wife.

By now, Mary Philips had arrived from New York and resumed film work after a five year gap. She freelanced in character parts in five films that were released in 1937, including *That Certain Woman* with Bette Davis and Henry Fonda at Warner Bros. But she realised that Mayo Methot had supplanted her in

Bogart's affections and that there was better work to be had on the stage, so she went back East and began divorce proceedings.

Kid Galahad was the first film Bogart started in 1937. Despite sparse screen time, Bogart contrived – on his first collaboration with director Michael Curtiz – to make a striking impression as a thoroughly nasty and humourless piece of work, a fights racketeer called Turkey Morgan. But then, unlike the other directors Bogart had previously encountered at Warners, Curtiz was a man of real talent and drive who worked hard at getting the most out of his players and their characters.

Bogart is memorably introduced walking in on a boisterous three-day party with a gang of thugs who chill the room to silence. When he proceeds to humiliate a bellhop by shortening his trouser legs with a flick-knife, no one dares intervene. It is this same bellhop (played by Wayne Morris) that the honest fights promoter Nick Donati (Edward G. Robinson) grooms into a contender for the heavyweight title held by Bogart's man. When the youngster dares to fall in love with Robinson's pure young sister (Jane Bryan), the promoter pushes him into a match with the champion (for which he's ill-prepared), and guarantees the result to Bogart. But Robinson has a change of heart and helps the kid win. The double-crossed Bogart goes down to the dressing-rooms to settle accounts with Robinson.

Here Curtiz inserts his familiar expressionistic directorial signature of shadows on a wall which show Bogart robbing a news photographer of his credentials and firing his gun into the crowd to draw off the police and reporters who, by surrounding the new champ's dressing-rooms, prevent him from reaching Robinson. Only when Robinson casually asks about the commotion do we learn just how ruthless Bogart is. His shot has struck a spectator – 'some insurance guy from

Ohio – first time in town'. The information about the victim is just specific enough to evoke some sympathy and thoroughly condemn Bogart's character. When Robinson enters the shower room, Bogart is waiting behind the door. Bogart manages to fatally wound Robinson in the shoot-out that follows but is himself killed. He makes the simple matter of dropping dead an attention-seizing affair as he crumples up in front of a wash basin in the shower room, his face contorted, with an arm across his chest, wrist curled after dropping his weapon, both hands coming loosely together in front of him. As the more important character, Robinson takes his time about expiring, having a deathbed speech to deliver.

By settling for a surly, tight-lipped malevolence, Bogart sacrificed colour and variety in favour of an intensity reinforced by the actor's splendid command of mean glares and lip-curling snarls; his stiffness of manner appropriately suggested the character's lack of flexibility. Having seen him play such a part, who would have thought that Bogart had any prospect of becoming a romantic leading man?

6

DEAD ENDS

Like *The Petrified Forest*, *Dead End* was a film version of
a Broadway play that thoughtfully probed the impact
of the gangster on American life. By playing Duke
Mantee, Bogart had proved that he knew how to
handle the part of a serious gangster, so he was an
obvious candidate for the role of Baby Face Martin in
Dead End and was borrowed from Warners by
producer Sam Goldwyn to work for director William
Wyler when production started in May 1938. To Lewis
Yablonsky, his authorised biographer, George Raft
described at some length how he was offered the role
but turned it down because Goldwyn and Wyler
wouldn't let him play it for sympathy. Apparently, this
was the first instance of what would become a custom;
that is, Bogart inheriting worthwhile parts refused by
Raft.

Martin is thirty-one years old with eight murders
behind him. He pays a nostalgic visit to the slum street
where he was born, protected from recognition by
plastic surgery. He is toying with the idea of settling
down with his ex-girlfriend, but he discovers that she
has become a prostitute. He also expects a warm
welcome from his mother (Marjorie Main), who
promptly slaps his face and denounces him, snarling,
'You dog, you dirty yellow dog, you! You ain't no son
of mine!' 'I killed a guy for looking at me the way you
are now!' Bogart hisses back at his mother. (Raft had
wanted to walk away with a tear in his eye.) The

character's subsequent reasoning is sharp and to the point: 'I came home for something. I didn't get it. I'm coming out with something – even if it's only dough.'

So Bogart recruits some of the slum kids to help him kidnap a rich youth. He incurs the wrath of Joel McCrea who has spent six years studying to become an architect and represents the best kind of slum product just as Bogart represents the worst. They are natural adversaries and when McCrea actually kills Bogart in hand-to-hand combat it is a symbolic victory of the builder over the destroyer. McCrea also earns a huge reward that will ensure him a bright future.

Bogart's Martin is a memorably ugly and touchy figure, more insidiously evil than most of the Hollywood gangsters of the Thirties, proud of his achievements but at the same time aware that he has reached a dead end both literally (the dead end street of the title) and figuratively, as his sentimental hopes for a new life are dashed.

Also on a loan-out from Warners, Bogart was reunited with Leslie Howard for a mild comedy about Hollywood called *Stand-In*. Based, like *Mr. Deeds Goes to Town*, on a story by Clarence Budington Kelland, it told a similar tale of a young innocent plunged into a strange and somewhat hostile environment and finding his feet with the help of a girl. Here it is Leslie Howard as the New York accountant investigating the finances of a movie studio with the help of the stand-in played by Joan Blondell. Bogart is Douglas Quintain, the production chief who has taken to the bottle since the break up of his romance with the studio's biggest star, Cherie (Marla Shelton). While Howard unearths a scheme involving Cherie and the studio's prize director, Koslofski (Alan Mowbray), to sabotage the studio and lower its selling price, Bogart provides the cutting-room skill to turn their feeble adventure picture into a hilarious comedy that will save the company. Bogart seemed to spend most of the time standing around holding a black Scottie; he had little chance to register, though he does gain a big laugh from audiences with the glance of sour disgust he gives Alan Mowbray after they have just had a private screening of his dreadful picture.

When Bogart returned to the Burbank lot, Warners seemed to have forgotten all about him and were at a loss to know what he should do next. He was absurdly cast in *Swing Your Lady*, which he later regarded as his worst film – and it probably was. He was wasted as a wrestling promoter called Ed Hatch, down on his luck and stranded in the wilds of Missouri, who comes up with the hare-brained idea of putting his wrestler (Nat Pendleton) against a powerful woman blacksmith (Louise Fazenda). The result was hillbilly farce.

Then, in January 1938, Jack Warner revealed his intention of recasting the Torchy Blane series of B films with Ann Sheridan and Humphrey Bogart. Glenda Farrell had played Torchy, the crime reporter, with Barton MacLane as her police detective boyfriend Steve McBride, in four films turned out by Bryan Foy's department. For Ann Sheridan, the part of Torchy would have been a reasonably promising step forward, but for Bogart to have gone into a series, and in a secondary role, would have been an irreversible backwards step.

In an interview with W.H. Mooring of the British *Film Weekly* (23 April 1938), the actor referred to the biggest drawback of the studio contract system: 'It is nice to have the weekly cheque, but there's nothing to provide for turning out a steady diet of good parts at a perfect pace for every contract player any studio has on its books. I had this fact in mind when I went to Mr. Warner with my complaint that I didn't think the Torchy series was right for me. I was prepared, as he probably knew, to compel the studio to suspend me, rather than go on with the idea ... Fortunately for me, however, Mr. Warner saw my point of view and relieved me of the weight. I got out of that before I got into it – and was I glad!' Warners cast Lola Lane and Paul Kelly in their next Torchy Blane movie, and when that didn't work Glenda Farrell and Barton MacLane were recalled for some further adventures.

It's interesting to read the editor of *Film Weekly*'s comments in the 29 January 1938 issue, on the proposal to put Bogart in the Torchy Blane pictures: 'Filmgoers, I believe, were expecting, as I was, to see Warners build Bogart into a second Paul Muni. He could be that, with more appeal and less theatricalism than Muni has developed. Instead they propose making him into one of dozens of competent heavy leading men. They should know that any actor's stock sinks like a stone when his name becomes associated with B pictures. Perhaps Warners are afraid Bogart has no romantic appeal. They might be interested in the ardour with which women in this country speak and write of him.'

Getting out of Torchy Blane, Bogart had little choice but to accept what he was offered, which was dire. In fact, *Men Are Such Fools*, the first of nine films he made in 1938, is beyond the pale. A 'sophisticated' comedy set in the advertising world with Bogart as an agency executive called Harry Galleon, it introduces him, after some twenty minutes, immersed in poolside chitchat with heroine Priscilla Lane. He falls for her and keeps her late at the office when she should be home with her husband (Wayne Morris). 'I'm probably a cad,' Bogart declares. 'Are you by any chance a weak woman? Oh, too bad. In that case I'll have to be a strong cad.' As if such dialogue wasn't bad enough, Bogart suffers the shame of being knocked to the ground by an irate Wayne Morris and staying there. But then Morris was the star, and Bogart had only third billing. The film was a test, really, of Bogart's integrity. When the parts were as insultingly trivial as this, he played them straight and to the best of his ability, when it would have been perfectly understandable for him to have hammed them up or to have said his lines half-heartedly.

After finishing *Men Are Such Fools*, Bogart went straight into another of Bryan Foy's confections at the beginning of February. This was *Crime School* and it proved something of a break for the actor, though more for the Dead End Kids who were the attraction that turned this modest main feature into an unexpectedly big box-office hit when it was released in June. Realising the wide appeal of these roughnecks in *Dead End*, Warners had signed them up and *Crime School* was the first of several films to display more of their antisocial antics. Bogart must have approached the reunion with some trepidation as on *Dead End* he had rubbed the gang up the wrong way on one occasion for which he had been divested of his trousers. And this time he wasn't trying to corrupt them but reform them.

The film was mostly a remake of James Cagney's 1933 *The Mayor of Hell* but it incorporated the romantic misunderstanding from *San Quentin* when Bogart falls in love with one of the kids' sister – Bryan Foy wasn't missing any chances. When Cagney had played it, he was a brash young hoodlum who is appointed to run a reformatory and wins the kids over by talking to them on their own level. Bogart wasn't youthful or volatile enough for that approach, and played a social worker named Mark Braden who is running the reformatory on progressive lines, much to the disgust of the tyrannical superintendent (Cy Kendall), who has his revenge by letting the kids believe Bogart is misbehaving with the sister. Her brother and some of the others break out and go after Bogart with a gun ... Bogart offered steady sincerity in the role and *Crime School* is one of his more rewarding pictures of this period.

Going on immediately into *The Amazing Dr. Clitterhouse*, Bogart had his gangster image amusingly sent up as criminologist Edward G. Robinson describes his Rocks Valentine as 'a magnificent specimen of pure viciousness'. Bogart does his best to live up to this estimate when to further his research into the criminal temperament, Robinson displaces him as the leader of a gang of thieves. Eventually Bogart drives Robinson to extend his experiments to murder, and the essentially comic tone of the film evaporates as Bogart, having downed a poisoned drink, struggles to remain conscious, Robinson keenly recording the details of his slow demise, then dispatching him to a watery grave. The film ends splendidly with Robinson's trial for Bogart's murder. By claiming he is perfectly sane Robinson persuades the jury that the opposite must be true, and is acquitted.

Bogart's next film, *Racket Busters*, was a brisk, minor drama on which he received top billing. Here was another of his misanthropic villains, called Martin, looking out over New York City by night, flashing his teeth in a mirthless smile and exclaiming 'Hello, suckers!' Bogart sets his gang to work muscling in on the fruit and produce market, then makes brief appearances from time to time, probably when he could be spared from the other film he had begun making. George Brent played the trucker who eventually rebels against Bogart's organisation, chasing him through an alleyway for the required showdown between hero and villain. Bogart now pays the price for having left the dirty work to his men: when he tries to gun down Brent, he shows himself to be out of practice (or maybe he always was a bad shot). He fires twice at close range, missing both times, and puts one bullet in the floor beside Brent's foot. The obligatory final scene shows Bogart, sulking and unrepentant, listening to the judge (Charles Trowbridge) denounce him as an enemy of society.

The film that Bogart was making simultaneously with *Racket Busters* was shot under the title *The Unlawful* but released as *King of the Underworld*. In this one Bryan Foy devised an ingenious way of remaking *Doctor Socrates* (1935), by giving Kay Francis the Paul Muni role of a doctor who outwits a gang of crooks. Bogart gained the part of the ruthless gang leader that Barton MacLane had previously undertaken. His Joe Gurney had some entertaining aspects: he captures a writer and commissions a biography that will flatter his vision of himself as a latter-day Napoleon (that idea came from Warners' 1930 gangster film, *Doorway to Hell*). Bogart meets his downfall when Kay Francis contrives to blind him temporarily with an eyedrop solution, and the police shoot him on a first floor landing. He tumbles down the stairs, clutches his bleeding chest, and makes a last request that no one should ever know that the new Napoleon was outwitted by a woman.

As this film finished, Bogart went straight into *Angels with Dirty Faces*. This was one of Warners' big pictures of 1938, which, at this stage of Bogart's career, meant that his role was a minor one. He was at his most slippery and shifty as lawyer James Frazier who welches on a deal to reward James Cagney for taking a three-year sentence for a crime they both committed. Cagney claims what's his at gunpoint and also takes some incriminating accounts to ensure his future safety. Bogart and his associate Mac Keefer (George Bancroft), think that Cagney has deposited the stolen papers with his priest friend (Pat O'Brien) and arrange to have the priest killed. Cagney overhears the plotters and calmly guns down Bogart who is reduced to plead for his life: 'Don't, don't, I'll do anything!' cries Bogart in one of his more craven departures. As with Barton MacLane in *Bullets or Ballots*, Bogart acted rings around George Bancroft whose elementary style meant that his only advantage was his size. Still, it was

Cagney who stole the picture, turning rotten coward on Death Row in order to discredit himself in front of the unruly Dead End Kids, who saw him as their role model.

On 20 August 1938, shortly after finishing *Angels with Dirty Faces*, Bogart married his third wife, Mayo Methot. She was doing small parts in two or three films a year, including an unnamed blonde in Warner Bros.' *The Sisters* which starred Errol Flynn and Bette Davis. Her father was a seaman and she shared Bogart's love for the sea: they had joined a yacht club and Bogart had a cruiser. But her relative inactivity in a childless marriage gave her time to develop the jealousy and drinking habit that would later wreck their relationship.

It was back to work for Bogart in another crime drama, filmed under the title *Crime Is a Racket* and released as *You Can't Get Away with Murder*. It is routine but undeniably entertaining. Bogart plays the part of Frank Wilson, a petty crook who kills a pawnbroker in a hold-up and is scared that his young accomplice (Billy Halop, one of the Dead End Kids) will give him away. They are both put in jail on another charge, and then the youngster starts to weaken. Bogart takes the boy with him on a jailbreak and shoots him, hoping to pass off the wounds as the result of police fire before he surrendered. But the youngster lives long enough to put Bogart in the electric chair.

In *The Oklahoma Kid*, Cagney and Bogart played contrasting kinds of Western badmen. Cagney was the Kid, a colourful rascal and a good guy at heart. Bogart was Whip McCord, the crooked boss of Tulsa City, dressed in black from head to foot. Bogart doesn't really have much to do, but from the introductory shot of him nodding his head thoughtfully as he watches a consignment of gold being unloaded from a train, he brings brooding presence to the role.

His first run-in with Cagney is entertaining. He steps

forward, puffing out his chest. 'My name's Whip McCord. Does that mean anything to you?' Cagney thinks a moment, then comments, 'I don't like it,' before turning to the man next to him to ask, 'Do you?'

After Bogart has incited a mob to lynch Cagney's law-abiding father, Cagney slips into the back of Bogart's saloon to settle the score. As he arrives on the first floor landing, Bogart hits him with a chair. They exchange a few blows and their doubles carry the fight downstairs by crashing through the bannisters in the traditional way. After some more action with chairs and broken bottles, Bogart attempts to plug his opponent and is shot dead. The film is a brisk affair with Bogart once again the perfect tinder for Cagney's explosive temperament.

In his autobiography, *Cagney by Cagney*, the star recalls Bogart 'doing his usual expert job' on *The Oklahoma Kid* and adds: 'By this time in his career he'd become entirely disillusioned with the picture business. Endlessly the studio required him to show up without his even knowing what the script was, what his dialogue was, what the picture was about. On top of this he would be doing two or three pictures at a time. That's how much they appreciated him. He came into the make-up department one morning and I said, "What is it today, Bogie?" "Oh, I don't know," he said. "I was told to go over to Stage Twelve." There he was fulfilling his contract, doing as required, however much against his will.' In fact, besides the Cagney picture, Bogart was finishing *Crime Is a Racket* (*You Can't Get Away with Murder*) and appearing in *Dark Victory*.

Bette Davis's favourite film, *Dark Victory* offers a rare example of Bogart's failure to enhance a picture. Woefully miscast as a brash, cheerful Irish groom, Michael O'Leary (a lock of hair curled forward on to his forehead to make him seem young enough for the part), he made a brave attempt at a brogue – but to no avail.

Fortunately, the part was not a sizeable one, providing him with only one major scene. In that, he strikes an artificial stance pouring out his frustrations to Bette Davis. 'What good's riding and fighting these days?' he asks angrily. 'Where do they get you?' Expressing his adoration for Davis, he seizes her boldly for a tight embrace, then apologises for his behaviour when she tells him she is doomed to an early death from a brain tumour. While she snatches some last months of happiness in marriage to her doctor (George Brent), Bogart pops up once more to remark on her healthy appearance, adding, 'It must be the prayers I've been saying,' and spoils her day by reminding her of what lies ahead. The character was quite as clumsy as Bogart's handling of it.

In February 1939, Bogart was assigned to another Bette Davis 'weepie', *The Old Maid*, with the same director, Edmund Goulding. The part of the lover who makes Davis pregnant and then dies in the Civil War was brief but significant, and difficult to cast. Bogart was given the part as a last resort to see how he fared. He was removed after shooting the scene at the railroad station because he didn't seem dashing enough, and George Brent replaced him. Again Bogart's romantic potential escaped the studio bosses, and he was pushed further into villainy with his weirdest role in *The Return of Doctor X*. Before that, however, he and his wife Mayo accompanied other stars on a special Hollywood train to Kansas for the world premiere of Errol Flynn's latest western, *Dodge City*, at all three of Dodge City's cinemas on 1 April. Stars from the film included Flynn, Ann Sheridan and Alan Hale, and Buck Jones, John Payne, Rosemary Lane and Jane Wyman, among others, also attended. On the train ride, Mayo attacked Bogart in the bar for talking to another woman.

No role ever gave Bogart better cause to blanch, both on-screen as a blood-starved vampire and off-screen than the one he played in *The Return of Doctor X*; Bogart claimed he only accepted it in exchange for an increase in salary. But once again he remained unruffled and made the most of the part. And, despite the ridicule usually attached to this film in surveys of the actor's career, it should be stated that it was actually a decent horror programmer (though not, despite its title, a sequel to Warners' big hit of 1932, *Doctor X*).

In it, Bogart plays Marshall Quesne, assistant to a famous haematologist (John Litel). The scene eerily lit, he makes his first appearance in the film in white laboratory gown, clutching a rabbit, and extending a cold, clammy hand to shake that of the hero-doctor (Dennis Morgan). His hair is streaked with white, he has a shiny marble pallor, speaks without emotion and has an excessively polite manner. At first Morgan advances the professional observation that Bogart is 'a strange looking creature'. Morgan later goes further, classifying his appearance as a 'cold graveyard look'. But then the level of scientific discussion has been set by John Litel himself, murmuring, 'Interesting stuff, blood,' as he shakes a few test tubes.

Bogart's character is eventually exposed as none other than the former 'medical genius', Dr. Francis Xavier, who was electrocuted by the state for letting his investigative zeal run away with him: he killed a baby in an experiment to see how long it could survive without food. Now Bogart, who was revived by Litel, can stay alive only by draining blood from suitable victims, one of whom (Rosemary Lane), he forces to his ramshackle laboratory in some misty swampland in New Jersey. As they drive along, he sits dressed in cloak and trilby flexing his gloved fingers and looking especially pasty faced. Rosemary Lane finally realises that her blood is going to put some colour back into his complexion. Fortunately, her boyfriend (Wayne Morris), and the police are hot on Bogart's trail and shoot him at the laboratory, terminating his brief incursion into territory normally reserved for Boris Karloff or George Zucco.

This was the only picture Bogart shot during the first half of 1939, but he made up for lost time and had worked on four more productions by the end of the year.

Directed by Raoul Walsh, *The Roaring Twenties* (begun as *The World Moves On*) was a bustling anthology of the gangster film's stock situations as evolved in the Thirties – beginning with a variation on the one about the boyhood chums who go their different ways in later life. In the opening scene, set on a World War I battlefield, Jeffrey Lynn nobly refuses to kill a German soldier who looks a mere boy of fifteen. Bogart, however, shows his character by looking along his rifle, squeezing the trigger and announcing, 'He won't be sixteen.' The third soldier, James Cagney, comes somewhere in between. He joins Bogart in the rackets of the Prohibition era when he can't find honest work, then drops out. He comes back to deal with Bogart when the latter threatens the life of Lynn, who also worked in the rackets but is now a crusading crime fighter. Bogart realises Cagney is a threat but is not quick enough to stop Cagney getting the drop on him. He raises his hands and retreats, quaking with fear, desperately grabbing an ornament to fling at Cagney who then shoots him. Sliding down the wall, he murmurs 'Crazy! Crazy!', before Cagney shuts him up for good with two more blasts from his gun.

As in *Oklahoma Kid* and *Angels with Dirty Faces*, Cagney and Bogart work in conflicting styles that enhance the drama: Cagney full of restless vitality, open and direct; Bogart more intense and controlled, his fury spilling out in sudden eruptions. Various incidents bring out this intense anger: when Bogart's last cigarette is knocked out of his hand by Cagney crashing down on him in the foxhole; when he recognises a bullying sergeant (Joe Sawyer) from his war days as a guard in the raid on the liquor warehouse and with a look of crazed glee pumps two bullets into him; and when he pulls out a gun to threaten Jeffrey Lynn, then calms down to issue a warning in the slick and gaudy patter that characterises the film: 'Listen, Harvard, you came into this racket with your eyes open. You know a lot, you learned a lot. If any of it gets out, you'll go out with your eyes open, only this time they'll have pennies on them!' In the scene on the liquor boat in which Cagney and Bogart forge their partnership, the former walks around while Bogart sits: it's partly the supporting player deferring to the star (the audience watches the one that moves), but is also indicative of their contrasting personalities.

Next on Bogart's agenda was to have been a starring role as a crusading reporter opposite Jane Wyman in a B picture for Bryan Foy called *Floating Troubles*. But, in another round of last-minute casting switches in mid-August, his role was given to Wayne Morris (the film came out under the title of *Gambling on the High Seas*). Bogart was needed for *Invisible Stripes*, which had undergone a casting shake-up after James Cagney had suddenly withdrawn from the starring role.

Invisible Stripes returned Bogart to the prison exercise yard. Under Lloyd Bacon's slack direction, he and George Raft play separate but identical scenes as convicts receiving the governor's standard lecture before they are released, through which Bogart devastatingly displays his superior acting ability. Raft provides an exaggerated picture of contrition and foolishly relaxes his usual deadpan demeanour; Bogart breezes in after him, barely concealing his contempt, the embodiment of hardened criminality. Subsequently, Raft tries to go straight but finds his 'invisible stripes' make it impossible. Bogart's Chuck Martin returns happily to a life of crime and welcomes Raft as a confederate in a series of bank hold-ups. Raft is acting altruistically, to make some money and keep his discontented younger brother (William Holden) from turning to crime. Bogart is not especially evil: crime is just his way of making a living. Both pay the price in the expected manner. Bogart came fourth in the cast, after Raft, Jane Bryan, and newcomer Holden. He was in fourth place yet again on his next picture.

Virginia City was a noisy, overblown Civil War Western, and Bogart again donned the black garments of villainy, sported a proper moustache for the second and last time in his screen career, and wrestled with a Mexican accent as a half-breed called John Murrell whose *beezness* is banditry. Errol Flynn represents the North, Randolph Scott stands for the Confederacy, and Bogart is the one who mistakenly tries to get the better of them, attempting to hold up Flynn and to relieve Scott of a gold shipment. The last is his fatal mistake. Bogart sounded like Speedy Gonzales and demonstrated again that accents were not his forte; besides which, the part really needed a genuine Mexican villain of the type that Hollywood subsequently discovered in Alfonso Bedoya. Miriam Hopkins was the romantic interest, billed ahead of Bogart.

In a whimsical oddity called *It All Came True*, Bogart was a gambler and night club operator who hides out from the police in a quaint boarding-house run by two sweet old ladies and largely occupied by non-paying guests from the theatrical profession who are permanently 'between engagements'. Bogart turns the place into a Gay Nineties club, puts the boarders back to work, and thereby reveals his whereabouts to the police. Ann Sheridan and Jeffrey Lynn were billed above Bogart as a singer and songwriter who help the show to succeed. Originally James Stewart was to have played Jeffrey Lynn's role.

Bogart began 1940 with *Brother Orchid*, one of the

Warner studio's periodic gangster spoofs. Like such predecessors as *Little Giant* and *A Slight Case of Murder*, it starred Edward G. Robinson as the gang leader who turns over a new leaf. Here he hands over to the boys, led by Humphrey Bogart's Jack Buck, and embarks on a European cultural spree. Destitute after five years of high living, he wires the gang to expect him back. Led by a smiling Bogart, they lay out the red carpet and usher him into his old seat at the head of the table, where they've wired up a little surprise to give him the news that he's through. Robinson tries setting up a rival mob and is nearly bumped off by Bogart. The film's comic highlights show Robinson taking refuge in a monastery and being converted to its way of life. However, Bogart isn't entirely forgotten: he gets such a grip on the city market that the monastery is unable to sell its flowers, so Robinson sets forth, corners Bogart and pounds him into surrender in a colourful fracas.

Given a rare sympathetic role as a happily married truck driver, Bogart inevitably seemed somewhat subdued in Raoul Walsh's vigorous melodrama, *They Drive By Night* (originally shown in Britain as *The Road to Frisco*). He and George Raft are brothers running a private haulage business and driving all hours to keep up the payments on their vehicle. Raft, a bachelor, enjoys the life and Bogart goes along with his views. Though he yearns to spend more time at home with his wife (Gale Page), he refuses her plea that he should allow their truck to be reclaimed by the finance company. But Bogart dozes off behind the wheel and wrecks the vehicle, losing an arm in the process. Thereafter, Bogart is only glimpsed, slowly rallying from a bout of depression, while Raft flirts with Ann Sheridan and is chased by Ida Lupino who murders her husband (Alan Hale), to make herself available for him. Eventually, Raft re-establishes himself in business, making Bogart his transport manager.

Above: In one of his early Fox films, *A Devil with Women* (1930), Humphrey Bogart gets tough with Michael Vavitch as the leader of revolutionaries in a banana republic. The lady is Mona Maris.

Above: This is Duke Mantee: Humphrey Bogart with cohorts Joe Sawyer (left), and Adrian Morris in *The Petrified Forest* (1936).

Above: In *Black Legion* (1937), Humphrey Bogart is recruited into the terror organisation and reluctantly accepts a gun he can ill-afford to buy.

Above: In *Marked Woman* (1937), Bogart as a prosecutor questions one of the girls who help him convict a crime czar. The actress is Mayo Methot whom Bogart subsequently married.

Above: James Cagney forces Bogart to make a phone call in *Angels with Dirty Faces* (1938).

Right: In his unlikeliest role as the vampire Doctor Francis Xavier in *The Return of Doctor X* (1939).

Left: Bogart, with Ida Lupino as the girl who really loves him, in *High Sierra* (1941).

Above: Gripping his cigarette, Bogart prepares to lay out his highly perfumed visitor, played by Peter Lorre, in *The Maltese Falcon* (1941).

Above: The stuff that dreams are made of – in *The Maltese Falcon* (1941), the titular object is admired by Peter Lorre, Mary Astor and Sydney Greenstreet while Bogart watches.

Above: In the climactic scene from *Across the Pacific* (1942), Bogart is held at gun point by Victor Sen Yung. Monte Blue and Mary Astor are the other captives.

Above: From the Parisian romance of Bogart and Ingrid Bergman, seen in flashback in *Casablanca* (1942).

Above: Bogart in discussion with Marcel Dalio's French patriot and underground leader in *To Have and Have Not* (1944), watched by Walter Brennan and Lauren Bacall.

Above: Bogart in a tender but possessive moment with Lauren Bacall in *The Big Sleep* (1946).

Humphrey Bogart and Lauren Bacall in *Dark Passage* (1947).

Bogart was again in fourth place in the cast list, just ahead of Gale Page (making her third film with him after *Crime School* and *You Can't Get Away with Murder*). He tried to upstage Raft by putting a match in his mouth until Raft objected, then trying a cigarette behind his ear instead, but Raft wouldn't let him get away with any distracting gestures. This was where nearly twenty years of acting had brought him, playing second-fiddle to a star he could act rings around. Yet, only four years later, he would be one of the Top Ten box-office draws.

7

THE TURNING POINT

In 1940, *High Sierra* gave Bogart a big break that might have come years earlier at any other studio. But the pecking order at Warners was so long that Bogart was only given roles that Cagney, Robinson, Raft, Garfield and Muni didn't want. All are said to have turned down the opportunity of playing Roy Earle in this W.R. Burnett–John Huston script: Raft because he didn't want to die and he didn't think his fans (or his mother) would like it; Muni because Raft had been offered it first and it didn't have a 'message'; and so on. Their loss was Bogart's gain, except that, despite having the major role, he had to take second billing to the fast-rising Ida Lupino.

The film is, quite simply, a glorification of the American gangster, a sentimental tribute on the occasion of his apparent passing from the American scene. It is here rather than in *The Petrified Forest* that Bogart earns Leslie Howard's toast as 'the last great apostle of rugged individualism'. Bogart's Earle is a completely sympathetic figure as the film pays no attention to the crimes that have put him in jail at the start of the film. He is sprung through the efforts of Big Mac (Donald MacBride), who is slowly dying and needs Bogart to carry out one last big caper for him. As Bogart walks out of prison, he rejects the seat in a waiting car and communes with nature (walking in a park, tossing a ball back to some kids) and with his past (a call at the farm where he was brought up). He befriends a simple, tiresome oldtimer (Henry Travers), who is taking his family across the country in an old jalopy and intervenes on their behalf when they cause a minor road accident.

Bogart is not only decent but loyal. He reassures MacBride: 'I never let nobody down – you know that.' Their reunion is more sad than joyful. 'All the good guys are gone – dead or in Alcatraz,' laments MacBride. 'Not many of the old bunch left,' comments the old doctor, played by Henry Hull. 'Sometimes I feel I don't know what it's all about any more,' Bogart declares.

When he later leads the raid on the Tropico Inn, working with youngsters he doesn't trust, he does it more to fulfil his obligation to MacBride than to resume a life of crime. He kills a policeman, but the policeman fired first and so it is (from Bogart's point of view, with which we identify) a case of self-defence. When Bogart subsequently finds himself labelled 'Mad Dog' Earle by the newspapers, he is disgusted and indignant; one is led to believe the bad image of gangsters was entirely a press invention.

Bogart is such a sentimental figure that he hasn't the heart to abandon a stray dog and he pays for a young girl (Joan Leslie), to be cured of a club-foot. He hopes that her gratitude will lead to love, as he idealises her beauty and youth. Her rejection of his marriage proposal is a hard blow especially as she chooses to marry a unprepossessing man in his middle years. Ironically Bogart's character is influenced by conventional standards of decency, and is slow to appreciate the real loyalty of Marie (Ida Lupino), the dance-hall girl who is deeply responsive to his kindness.

In the end, in keeping with the sympathetic treatment of Bogart's character, his noble qualities are his undoing. He refuses to be reimbursed by the crippled girl's fiancé for the operation and so has no funds to buy petrol; this forces him to hold up a store and put the police on his tail. Cornered in the mountains of the High Sierras, he responds to the barks of the stray dog racing up towards him and comes out far enough to be picked off by a marksman. It is this sharpshooter who carries out the film's real act of heroism, calmly climbing where no one has ever climbed before to get his sights on Bogart (though, of course, shooting him in the back does diminish the achievement). As Bogart lies dead, the dog licks his hand, Ida Lupino caresses it, and bystanders comment that he doesn't look so tough any more. Weeping bitterly, Lupino has the consolation that Bogart has 'crashed out' to freedom in the next world.

Why, one might ask, is this specious and maudlin picture so effective? One reason is that Raoul Walsh's direction does not dwell on the sentimental side but remains detached, and emphasises conflict, pace and action. Another is that Bogart never plays for pathos. In fact, Bogart's performance is remarkably astute. Far from a glamorous figure, he looks older than his actual years in a dark, crumpled suit, battered felt hat, loose collar, and severe prison haircut, but his Roy Earle is an unsentimental fellow, without self-pity, who keeps going, surrendering neither to the police nor to an introspective awareness of his symbolic function.

High Sierra's fondness for its tragic gangster hero mirrors the audience's basic liking for the genre, especially today when people think of the remote Thirties with nostalgia. We are not compelled to make moral judgements, not seriously anyway, so the film offers much to enjoy.

In real life, Humphrey Bogart was very discontented with his career and his private life, and it showed in his reputation as 'Bogie the Beefer', always carrying a big chip on his shoulder. Ida Lupino claimed he was abusive towards her during the shooting of *High Sierra*. In her case, his attitude may have been aggravated by the top billing she had in the picture.

James Cagney noticed: 'Not many people liked him, and he knew it. He said, "I beat 'em to it … I don't like them first." He hated just about everybody, but that was his aim – to hate them first. When it came to fighting, he was about as tough as Shirley Temple.'

And in *Starmaker*, Warners' producer and executive Hal Wallis observed: 'He was as much the tough guy at home, in his dressing-room, or in my office as he was on the sound stage. He drove a hard bargain, and every time he made a picture, he wanted an increase in salary.'

Now Bogart has become a cult figure, it has often been suggested that he cultivated this abrasive image for its publicity value. For example, he talked about his behaviour in a 1938 *Photoplay* interview: 'Nobody, *nobody* likes me on sight. I suppose that's why I'm a heavy, or vice versa. There must be something about the tone of my voice, or this arrogant face – something that antagonises everybody. I can't even get into a mild discussion that doesn't turn into an argument.'

His rows with his wife Mayo were so public that he could hardly hide them. He nicknamed her 'Sluggy' and she was reputed to have slung highballs at him, punched him on the nose, flung her fur coat at him when she found him talking to a couple of female fans, and on one occasion is said to have stabbed him with a knife. One evening she tracked him down at Chasen's restaurant after closing time while he was sitting talking to Dave Chasen, Jimmy Cagney and John Steinbeck. Recalled Cagney: 'Suddenly there was a loud banging at the back door. Chasen went there and it was Mayo Methot … Bogart excused himself and went back to talk with her. He returned a few minutes later. From what I had heard about their fights, I expected him to be torn and bloody, but he was unscathed and was laughing. What amused him was her parting line, which was "You and your goddamned drunken friends." The funny part was that all of us were sober. Nobody had a single drink.'

Bogart's only real choice was to play up these incidents and pretend he enjoyed them. Perhaps he did. 'There was no particular reason for these onslaughts: they were based on unfounded jealousies,' wrote Hal Wallis. 'I believe Bogie enjoyed the fights. He always wanted to seem as tough as possible.'

According to Raoul Walsh, who had previously directed Bogart in *They Drive By Night*, Bogart moaned so continuously about the food and accommodation on location for *High Sierra*, that Walsh pulled his leg by making out there was no lunch one day while they were high up in the mountains near Mount Whitney. Then, when the lunch box finally arrived, Bogart said its contents were worse than prison food. Walsh recalled: '[Bogart's] acting experience resembled that of John Barrymore; both hated, or appeared to hate, every part of the motion picture industry. John damned it because of the long hours and Bogie echoed him: "They get you up before daybreak and work your ass off all day until sundown. In the theatre I went to work at eight in the evening and was through by eleven; all the rest of the night and next day to play and catch up with my drinking. Working in pictures is for the birds." Bogart could go on like this indefinitely, and his invective never faltered.'

When Walsh pointed out how much better paid he was by the movies, Bogart's answer came with a scowl: 'That's the only kick I get out of this business.' Even then, as Hal Wallis has recalled, 'Bogie was always short of money. The studio files on him are full of requests by his agent, Sam Jaffe, for more money.' Bogart probably did need the money, as life with Mayo was obviously expensive and he was also supporting his mother who had come to Hollywood (until her death in 1940), as well as one of his sisters whose marriage had failed.

Despite Bogart's surly attitude, Walsh readily acknowledged that the actor gave fine performances in his pictures, and that his frustration with the treatment he was receiving at Warner Bros. was understandable. Taken with his marital difficulties, he had a lot to contend with.

Bogart had renewed cause to gripe when he was put into another routine picture, *The Wagons Roll at Night*. This was an ingenious reworking of *Kid Galahad* with Bogart's gangster role eliminated, the boxing background changed to a travelling carnival, and Bogart stepping up into Edward G. Robinson's former lead role. Here the emphasis was more on the leading character's Achilles' heel: his latent incestuous regard for his younger sister whom he has had raised in a convent to keep her 'clean and decent'. He regards the entertainers who work in his carnival as 'roadshow vermin', unfit to have any contact with her. When a young lion-tamer (Eddie Albert, equivalent to the boxer in *Kid Galahad*) falls in love with her, and Bogart's own girl, a fortune-teller (Sylvia Sidney), takes a shine to the lad, Bogart plots to send him unarmed into a cage with a killer lion. In a last minute change of heart, he rushes forward and is mauled instead: a few dark smudges on his face and a collar torn open suggest his fatal injuries. He survives long enough to speak to both his sister and the fortune-teller, regretting his jealousy and blessing his sis's romance with the lion-tamer.

As usual, Bogart wasn't content to walk through the part; he took it seriously and made something intense out of it. A confident manipulator of people, a devious schemer desirous of revenge, this character's lips curl as he registers several looks of distilled hatred. There are memorable images of him with his eyes glinting as the maddened lion roars nearby and baring his teeth like the beast Eddie Albert's lion-tamer will have to face with an empty gun. But he has more sympathetic moments when, for example, he realises that he might lose Sylvia Sidney, having come to depend on her support. Bogart's efforts were more than the picture deserved, with its nonchalant direction by Ray Enright and incongruous cheerful music which accompanies most of the dramatic moments (as though the score had been lifted indiscriminately from other movies).

One of the rigours of a studio contract was that even leading players could be sent out to make publicity appearances, not necessarily in connection with their own films or even their own studio's output. In Bogart's case, he and Mayo were sent to join the regular stage show at Warner Bros.' New York flagship theatre, the Strand, from 6 December 1940, with the hope of boosting business during the traditional pre-Christmas lull. *The Letter*, with Bette Davis, had already opened there with radio favourites Ozzie Nelson, his Orchestra and his wife Harriet Hilliard live on stage, and Bogart made personal appearances for the last two weeks of the film's four-week run. A montage of his death scenes played on the screen, the lights went up to reveal him stretched out on the stage, and then he got up, dusted himself off and remarked, 'One hell of a way to make a living!' before going into his routine. He was popular with urban audiences and his stint almost halted a drop in the Strand's takings, so Warner Bros. did know what they were doing. Then Bogart had to spend a week in early January, again with Ozzie Nelson, boosting business at another Warner Bros. theatre, the Earle, in Philadelphia. Here the film attraction, *Escape to Glory*, wasn't even a Warner Bros. picture but at least Bogart could offer some first-hand reminiscences about its star, his old colleague Pat O'Brien.

To Warners' credit, they had recognised the impact Bogart and Lupino had in *High Sierra* before it opened and in early 1941 wanted to reunite them in *Out of the*

Fog. But Lupino strongly opposed the idea of working with Bogart again (though in later years they became good friends – she declared she had mistaken his wry, moody behaviour for sarcasm before noting he only behaved that way with people he liked ...).

Lupino won – she meant more to the studio, and Bogart was replaceable. The male lead in *Out of the Fog* went to John Garfield, and Bogart was put into *Manpower* (or *Handle with Care* as it was then known), supporting Marlene Dietrich and George Raft. Then a derogatory remark that Bogart was supposed to have made to Raft's stand-in during a test led to Raft refusing to make the film if Bogart remained in it. Bogart was again replaceable. Hal Wallis gave his part to Edward G. Robinson. The temperamental Raft didn't hit it off with Robinson either, swearing at him and assaulting him in one of the most widely reported set disputes ever (which Warners, of course, regarded as wonderful publicity).

Within days of leaving *Manpower*, Bogart was handed a thoroughly demeaning assignment to keep him busy – playing Cole Younger in a routine western, *Bad Men of Missouri*, to be directed by Ray Enright. He sent the script back with a memo that read: 'Are you kidding – This is certainly rubbing it in – Since Lupino and Raft are casting pictures maybe I can ... Regards, Bogie.' He was put on suspension without salary while Dennis Morgan undertook Cole Younger. Fortunately, George Raft came to Bogart's rescue in June when he refused to make *The Maltese Falcon* with John Huston because he thought it wasn't an important enough picture, being a low-budget remake, and he didn't fancy entrusting his great talent to a first-time director.

Bogart took over the role of private investigator Sam Spade. This must have been what he had in mind when talking to the studio's aspiring actress Geraldine Fitzgerald. She recalled in 1965, 'Humphrey Bogart always told me that movies are like a slot machine – if you played long enough, you'd eventually hit the jackpot.' Ironically, she turned down the role of Brigid O'Shaughnessy which could have been her jackpot.

At last Bogart had found a part that really called for the particular qualities he could offer, including, at that time, a basic ambiguity about his moral position. Bogart seemed to be the hero but didn't always act like it, and was stamped, in the eyes of screen audiences, as a villain.

The Maltese Falcon is a particularly honest detective film. Like the later *The Big Sleep*, it restricts us (with fleeting exceptions) to scenes in which Bogart participates, so that we uncover the facts as he does, and can watch him closely to see how he responds to them. Unlike *The Big Sleep*, however, the plot eventually makes complete sense, if you care to work it out.

Bogart as Spade is decent enough to earn the uncritical devotion of his sensible secretary Effie (Lee Patrick), who mothers him and receives his confidences, yet he is not above having an affair with his partner's wife (Gladys George), nor is he particularly disturbed when his partner is murdered, losing no time in removing the man's desk and name from the office. As he gains a foothold in the main intrigue and learns about the precious, jewel-encrusted, golden Maltese falcon, he names himself as an interested party in sharing the spoils. After it falls into his hands, he delivers the 'black bird' to Gutman (Sydney Greenstreet), and the others, but whether he is working for monetary gain or to clear up the case is a debatable point. 'Don't be so sure I'm as crooked as I seem to be,' he declares at one point, and at the end he indicates that solving his partner's murder is a factor motivating his conduct. Bogart certainly succumbs to the atmosphere of greedy excitement that surrounds the prized object. He exultantly grips Effie's wrist until it hurts when receiving the falcon from the dying

Captain Jacobi, and he savours the thrill that Gutman and his colleagues derive from unwrapping the falcon after he has handed it over to them.

In the far from negligible 1931 version, Ricardo Cortez played Sam Spade as a suave ladies' man who lived and worked in plush surroundings. Here Bogart is an older figure with none of the romantic aura he was later to acquire. His nondescript clothes, his spacious, sunny but bare office, his gloomy and anonymous apartment – these give us an impression of a man who has got little from life. He is interested in Brigid O'Shaughnessy (Mary Astor) as a client because she is an alluring and classy dame who is clearly involved in something far bigger than the small-time work he normally handles.

When she asks how she can keep his help when she has no money, Bogart seizes her for a kiss. His brutish manner – putting his hands around her neck, pressing his thumbs into her cheeks, holding her head still for the kiss – was to become his standard technique as a screen lover, but here it suggests a certain crude eagerness and a lack of sophistication rather than the possessiveness of other films. Later Bogart determines to extract the truth about the falcon from her but he allows himself to be diverted into making love. At the end of the film, Bogart stampedes the truth out of her which is that she is a cold-blooded murderess. Here, his acting reaches its greatest intensity as his reasoning battles with his emotions, and he denies the burning impulse to save her as she implores him to do. His angry 'I won't play the sap for you,' contrasts with his melancholic 'I hope they don't hang you, precious, for that sweet neck,' (he gently touches it) and his consoling 'If they hang you, I'll always remember you.' Aided by the harsh lighting, Bogart looks really haggard as he speaks of the sleepless nights he'll have until time erodes the pain of losing her. His final decision – 'I won't because all of me wants to' – carries

71

a hint of indignation that he should have come so close to surrendering to impulse, but the overall tone is one of savage bitterness.

Throughout, Bogart's performance is tremendously alert, and scene after scene is enhanced by his handling of details. His toothy smile as he takes Brigid's excessively large retainer in his office; his humorous mimicking of Peter Lorre's Joel Cairo as he accepts money from him ('I will take, say, two hundred'); his effort to shake himself awake as the telephone pierces the still of night with the news of his partner's death; the puzzled reaction to a drugged drink as he shakes his head and tries to remain conscious; the way he turns his head slowly to look at Brigid after one of Gutman's remarks shows her to him in her true colours, and the subsequent smile he gives her as he gently relieves her of the gun he now knows she is fully capable of using: all these and more contribute to a remarkably rounded impression we gain of Sam Spade. Had the part been played as flatly as George Raft would have handled it, *The Maltese Falcon* would have become heavy going with its complications of plot, whereas Bogart fully maintains the interest of the audience because he makes Spade so interested in the other characters. His interest meshes perfectly with the marvellous performances contributed by the rest of an extraordinary cast.

On finishing *Falcon*, Bogart went straight into yet another film that George Raft had refused to make, *All Through the Night*, but for once Raft's suspicions had been well-founded. It wasn't a particularly good part and Bogart undertook it with reluctance, having his agent, Sam Jaffe, write to Warners asking that future roles should be conceived specifically for him.

Nevertheless, *All Through the Night* demonstrated an improvement in Bogart's standing: he was now the leading man in a big picture, indeed the only star name in the cast. If the part of Broadway gambler Gloves Donahue wasn't tailored for his abilities, these were in the process of being established now that he was relieved of playing villains. The studio tried for a more youthful look – he sported a fuller head of hair – and gave him some athletic heroics in this spirited contribution to the war effort. It was a merry, Runyonesque comedy, directed by Vincent Sherman, pitting Bogart and his cronies against a band of Fifth Columnists plotting acts of sabotage. Bogart starts out nonchalant about world affairs: 'That's Washington's racket – let them handle it,' but refutes the argument of the Nazi (Conrad Veidt), that they should work together as neither has any respect for democracy. Bogart admits that he may not be a model citizen but points out that he pays his taxes and buys tickets for the policemen's ball.

Eventually Bogart becomes democracy's advocate before his sceptical fellow gamblers and even impresses shady Barton MacLane with the news that the Fascists would dictate what paper he could read. 'Why, that's against the law!' exclaims the veteran screen lawbreaker. The film substitutes speed for subtlety, and some good scenes – such as the one in which Bogart, forced to address a Nazi meeting as a supposed agent, stalls for time by talking gibberish – are rather buried in the rush. But a powerful supporting cast, including Jane Darwell, improbably cast as Bogart's domineering mother, help the actor put the action across in a pleasant and entertaining manner.

Following the success of *Falcon*, John Huston was promoted to director of a major production, *In This Our Life*, with Bette Davis starring. As a gesture of good luck, most of the *Falcon* cast – Bogart, Mary Astor, Peter Lorre, Sydney Greenstreet, Elisha Cook Jr., Barton MacLane and Ward Bond – came onto the film's roadhouse set and played extras. If you look closely enough, they are apparently visible in the background.

With *The Big Shot*, Bogart was again the sole box-office draw, his name on a separate title-card ahead of the main title. As in *High Sierra*, he played a sympathetic bad guy. His Joseph 'Duke' Berne receives a mandatory life sentence for his fourth offence – a hold-up he was in fact prevented from committing when his old girlfriend (Irene Manning), now the wife of the lawyer behind the job, detained him at gunpoint for his own good (a fade glosses over how she manages to keep him there).

It's a film spoilt by over-emphasis, with director Lewis Seiler exaggerating the contrasts as though he were handling a B-movie. There's the excessively forlorn Bogart to start, a three-time loser shuffling around the neighbourhood unshaven, spat on by cops, and goaded into taking part in the robbery by his old gang. There's the naive kid (Richard Travis), who messes up his alibi, and is forever apologising when they're cell-mates. He tries to prevent Bogart's escape, only to be convicted of the murder of a guard killed by Bogie's accomplice in the jailbreak.

Having escaped, Bogart embarks upon a life of domestic bliss with Irene Manning's character, in a sunny country cottage hideaway – idyllic images from Norman Rockwell of Bogart chopping the firewood and helping his girlfriend to mix the batter for buckwheat cakes, light music playing on the radio.

But, despite his hard-boiled background, this Bogart has the kid's fate on his conscience: 'All my life, I've only had one idea in my head – if a guy did anything for anybody else, he's a sucker. Now look at me, worrying about a kid I hardly even know.' Surprisingly, Manning worries about the kid, too, arguing they can never be happy unless they help him beat the murder rap. Unfortunately, the kid and his fiancée

(Susan Peters), are played so wetly that they fail to engage the sympathies of the audience. In the high-speed climax Bogart races with the cops to reach the warden. There's one moment in the hectic chase around slippery mountain roads when Bogart shows his vicious side. Seeing one of the pursuing motorcycle cops take a bad spill over a bank as Bogart outdistances them he chortles, 'That's one guy that won't make it any more! Suckers! We made it!' But this gloating is immediately quashed as he discovers that Manning has died next to him, hit by a police bullet.

There's some splendid touches of film noir in Sid Hickox's masterful cinematography, for example during Bogart's nocturnal visit to the lawyer who has disclosed the location of their hide-out. Bogart shoots him but is wounded himself and struggles back to the prison, to clear the kid and die with the shadow of prison bars across his face. *The Big Shot* is, understandably, one of the lesser known pictures of Bogart's star years.

For his third film as a director, John Huston had a proper reunion with Bogart, Mary Astor and Sydney Greenstreet in *Across the Pacific*, which began shooting in late November 1941. It was a laboured but entertaining attempt to recapture the success of *The Maltese Falcon*.

Playing a character called Rick Leland, Bogart teases audiences for a while by being court-martialled out of the Army and cultivating the friendship of Greenstreet, a Japanese agent, as both journey on a freighter to the Far East, but he soon revealed himself as the undercover agent we always thought he was.

Mary Astor was another woman of mystery, certainly not all she pretends to be, and Bogart directly echoes his dialogue to her in *The Maltese Falcon* by complimenting her, 'You're good, angel, you're very, very good,' before demanding the truth. Their romance is important to Bogart, who describes her as the kind of woman a young man dreams about, but it is mainly handled as sophisticated comedy. Bogart displays a deftness with lines that enable him to be knowingly comic and exasperating, but the dialogue is far from brilliant. Sydney Greenstreet complicates the plot and thoroughly outsmarts Bogart, leaving him unconscious on the floor, just as in *Falcon*, and beaten savagely with a walking stick (to correspond with Elisha Cook Jr.'s kicks to his face in the earlier film).

But the plot never amounts to enough to engage real interest and is spoiled by lack of thought. Bogart saves Greenstreet from an assassin's bullet and gains his trust but in the process consigns the thwarted killer to a quick execution (which surely ought to have left its mark on Bogart's conscience). The film climaxes with Bogart behind a machine-gun for some Errol Flynn-type heroics mowing down the 'Jap hordes' and putting an end to a far-fetched scheme to bomb the Panama Canal.

There were two particular problems in making the film. Production started just before the attack on Pearl Harbor, which was the original target in the film's script. The picture had to be put on hold while the story was relocated to Panama. And, just before shooting was completed, Huston received an urgent phone-call while on the set, from an army colonel. He had been summoned immediately to Washington to join the Signal Corps. He was working on the scene in which Bogart is taken prisoner and gleefully made it as impossible as he could for Bogart's character to escape from the clutches of the Japanese. As he recalled in Gerald Pratley's *The Cinema of John Huston*: 'I had Bogart bound to the chair, and then I put automatic weapons into everybody's hands. I made the ring of captors into three rings, and put people outside the windows with guns pointing at him. It had been decided that Vincent Sherman would take over for me.

It would now be up to Vincent to get him out of this! I spent the rest of the day making it utterly impossible for Bogart to make a false move without getting shot. Well, I saw the picture some time after the war and it lost credibility from that moment on!'

Sherman toiled for days with a mass of writers to work out a solution and, as Huston noted, the results were not very satisfactory. Yet even greater writing problems attended Bogart's next picture. They however, were resolved to everybody's lasting satisfaction.

8

A CLASSIC CALLED CASABLANCA

Casablanca is, of course, *the* film for which Bogart will always be remembered and the quintessential expression of the Bogart persona. Despite being created under the most extraordinary conditions of haste and confusion – new pages of script delivered days and weeks into shooting and players uncertain of the ending – it has the look of a thoughtfully prepared, lovingly crafted romantic melodrama. With a dazzling cast, it never wastes a second under Michael Curtiz's characteristically swift direction. The result remains a richly satisfying film, both of its time as rousing anti-Nazi propaganda, and timeless in its feeling for the vicissitudes of love.

As Rick Blaine, Bogart was no forthright screen hero but a touchy, stubborn, self-centred figure who couldn't always be relied upon to do the right thing. Yet the film also gave a whole new romantic dimension to Bogart, playing a man who has flung himself wholeheartedly into love and is immensely vulnerable. From a figure whose few leading ladies had tended to be on the mature side, he became a suitable romantic lead for the much younger Ingrid Bergman, reputedly because all the regular romantic leads were tied up – many were fighting the war. Despite legend, Ronald Reagan was never seriously considered to play Rick; it was either Raft or Bogart from the start. Astute for once, Raft asked for the part, but Bogart was chosen and the script was written with him in mind.

Casablanca's flashback shows us a sunny Parisian romance. Bogart is radiantly happy in his whirlwind courtship of Ingrid Bergman's Ilsa Lund, rushing her towards marriage, blind to the troubled look in her eyes and the hesitation in her voice. Her cryptic note of farewell as he hastens from Paris ahead of the German invaders is a stunning blow to his self-esteem as the symbolism of the rain suggests. It wipes out the episode by smudging Bergman's cruel, curt letter and implies Bogart's tears of grief.

Previously called Richard Blaine, he becomes 'Rick' of Rick's Place in Casablanca and by late 1941 he has hardened like his first name, withdrawing into himself, he is a changed man. When Yvonne (Madeleine LeBeau) seeks to extend what has obviously been a casual affair by asking where he'll be that evening, Bogart's reply, 'I never make plans that far ahead,' echoes Bergman's 'That's too far ahead to plan,' when he urged marriage on her at the earliest opportunity in Paris. When Bogart sharply rebuffs Sydney Greenstreet's attempt – as the black market leader, Signor Ferrari – to buy the services of the club pianist, Sam (Dooley Wilson), his reply reflects both his distaste for the city's ready bartering of human lives and his eagerness to keep Sam, his companion from his Paris days, as a ready reminder of the past which haunts him daily.

The film economically conveys Bogart's political inclinations despite his professed neutrality. He has fought the Fascists in Spain, and had to leave Paris because the Germans were keen to capture him. His recognition of the type of artillery heard booming in the Parisian suburbs is a clever indication of his military background. Even in Casablanca, he shows a strong and undiplomatic dislike for Germans, ordering one away from his gambling tables and letting the band play 'La Marseillaise' to drown out the Germans singing 'Die Wacht am Rhein', an act which leads to the closure of his club. Bogart is visibly impressed at the mention of the resistance leader, Victor Laszlo, and the Prefect of Police (Claude Rains), realises he will be tempted to help Laszlo escape to the free world. Bogart's attitude – 'I stick my neck out for nobody' – is clearly a case of self-deception. When he refuses to help the crook Ugarte (Peter Lorre) evade capture by the police, it is because it is too late to aid him as he did earlier by hiding his valuable letters of transit (irrevocable papers that will provide whoever carries them with the perfect means of escape from Casablanca). As Ugarte is carried off screaming, Rick reiterates 'I stick my neck out for nobody,' but there was nothing he could have done.

Thus almost everything predisposes Bogart to aid Laszlo (played by Paul Henreid). The stumbling block is Bergman's reappearance as Laszlo's companion. She asks Sam to play the tune that recalls Paris, 'As Time Goes By'. Bogart is furious with Sam for playing the forbidden song, then dumbfounded to see Bergman standing there. Next he breaks his rule of not drinking with customers by having a drink with her and Henreid.

Drinking late at night in a haze of cigarette smoke, he relives the past to help him resist the explanation for her betrayal that he knows she will bring, suspicious that she will only be seeking the letters of transit. It is a losing battle for both of them, and when Bergman ultimately seeks to take the precious letters at gunpoint, then breaks down, Bogart is forced to admire her once more, and then to accept her complete submission to his will. Paul Henreid's Laszlo seems a poor lover compared with Bogart: the very qualities of aloofness and cautious diplomacy that make him a 'great man' mean that he lacks spontaneity, reckless vitality and passion, though he needs Bergman's emotional support. His selfless offer to sacrifice his own freedom to ensure hers is noble, but cold-blooded and calculated.

For Bogart's Rick, the time has come to act, not react. His ingenious solution to everybody's problems teases us with the possibility that he has betrayed the resistance leader to the police, then enables him to 'play again' that unsatisfactory departure from Paris in the urgent departure scene at Casablanca's airport, again losing Bergman, but by his choice this time and so with his self-esteem intact. He has now 'betrayed' her, and yet strengthens their bond by doing it for the same reason she betrayed him: the greater cause embodied in Henreid's Laszlo.

And, in this thoroughly beguiling film, the climax is especially satisfying for two reasons: firstly because Bogart is given the opportunity to kill the Nazi leader (Conrad Veidt), after he has honourably but improbably allowed the German to get off the first shot; and secondly because the uncertainties of loving a woman are replaced with the more stable, less taxing friendship between two men – Bogart and Claude Rains, fellow patriots who thoroughly enjoy each other's company. That famous last line of Bogart's, 'Louis, I think this is the beginning of a beautiful friendship' – now one of the two or three most celebrated exit lines in the history of film – was devised (apparently by Hal Wallis) and added in post-production.

Bogart and Bergman made an explosive romantic combination on-screen, but off-screen it was a different matter. For one thing, Mayo Methot was around, looking for trouble, while, in her autobiography, *My Story*, Bergman recalled that Bogart was so cross at the lack of a proper script that he spent much of the time in his trailer. 'I'd hardly got to know Humphrey Bogart at all. Oh, I'd kissed him, but I didn't know him. He was polite naturally, but I always felt there was a distance: he was behind a wall. I was intimidated by him. *The Maltese Falcon* was playing in Hollywood at the the time and I used to go and see it quite often during the shooting of *Casablanca*, because I felt I got to know him a little better through that picture.'

Because Bogart concerned himself with the overall quality of a picture, he held up production at times, arguing with Curtiz over particular scenes, and one of the writers, Howard Koch, has recalled that Bogart once invited him into his trailer for a drink to discuss the script.

Casablanca had the colossal good fortune of being boosted by real life events. Allied Forces landed on the coast of North Africa on 8 November 1942 and took Casablanca. Warners considered revising the movie to include this development, then announced they were rushing a print just as it was to Casablanca for the Allied forces to enjoy. They also fixed a New York premiere before the month was over, but it wasn't until January that it went into general release, when Roosevelt and Churchill created more publicity by holding a conference in the town of the title. In February the film became the top attraction nation-wide, and it was sixth in the year's top ten at the box-office (behind *This Is the Army*, *For Whom the Bell Tolls*, *Random Harvest*, *Stage Door Canteen* and *Star-Spangled Rhythm*). More importantly for Bogart, its success turned him into a major new star. He was in the top ten box-office draws for 1943, behind Betty Grable, Bob Hope, Abbot and Costello, Bing Crosby, Gary Cooper and Greer Garson; and one step ahead of James Cagney. His work in *Casablanca* even gained him an Academy Award nomination for best actor but he lost to Paul Lukas, who also fought the Fascists (but more seriously) in another Warner film, *Watch on the Rhine*. (*Casablanca* did win the main Oscar for the Best Picture of 1943, and Michael Curtiz was named Best Director.)

Ingrid Bergman rejoined Bogart for a half-hour radio adaptation of *Casablanca*, broadcast on CBS on 26 April 1943, in the *Lady Esther Screen Guild Players* series (Lady Esther was a brand of cosmetics). During the 1940s Bogart did more than a dozen radio shows, not all of them adaptations of his films. In 1943, he was also heard in thirty-minute versions of *Across the Pacific* and *The Maltese Falcon*, in both cases with Mary Astor and Sydney Greenstreet, while in 1950 he repeated *Falcon* with Lauren Bacall.

Warners developed plans to reunite Bogart and Bergman in a new screen version of *A Farewell to Arms* and purchased the rights from Paramount but, before the film was made Bogart had formed the even more potent partnership with Lauren Bacall, which didn't suit the material. (The studio eventually remade the story as *Force of Arms* [1951] with William Holden and Nancy Olson. However, in another of his radio appearances, Bogart starred opposite Joan Fontaine in a one-hour adaptation of the Hemingway novel for *The Theatre Guild on the Air*, broadcast on 22 October 1950.)

Two other war films helped Bogart attain the heights of the box-office top ten during 1943. He shot the first, *Action in the North Atlantic*, directly after *Casablanca*, between September and December 1942. This was a propaganda movie, rushed into production to boost the Merchant Marine, then suffering huge losses from U-boat attacks. Despite its maritime setting, the players did all their work on the studio sound stages.

Any rugged actor from the studio ranks could have played Bogart's part of first mate Joe Rossi on a merchant ship making hazardous Atlantic crossings during wartime as, despite solo billing ahead of the title, he largely plays a subordinate role to Raymond Massey's Captain Jarvis. Bogart plays a simple-minded, fun-loving fellow who has to be rescued from the women he meets by Massey. Then he silences a loudmouth who interrupts the singer in an empty bar and ends up married to her. At sea, he is conscientious, respectful and considers himself too undisciplined to command. He has sailed into Axis ports and doesn't like what he sees, but isn't enormously steamed up about it.

The film depicts how he changes under the pressure of events. When Massey is wounded he becomes an able captain, successfully operates on Massey's leg, outwits a German submarine and conducts a funeral service with quiet dignity, emphasising the obligation that the living have to the dead to honour the sacrifices made by them. As their international convoy reaches the Russians Bogart strangely casts a shadow across the celebratory tone of the sequence by contemplating the hazards of the journey back.

The film is excellent war propaganda, and the action scenes are its most memorable aspect. One particular sequence, in which the characters played by Bogart and Massey are caught up in smoke and explosions on a sinking freighter, required some spectacular stuntwork by the actors' doubles. Bogart and Massey were on the sidelines watching, and Bogart remarked: 'You may be a better actor than I am, Ray, but my double is braver than yours.' According to Massey, he and Bogart then took over from their doubles and did the scene, which required that they descend from the burning bridge of the boat to the flaming deck and slide down ropes into a lifeboat. Bogart suffered singed eyebrows.

The other war film in which audiences saw Bogart in 1943 was *Sahara*. He made it early in the year at Columbia as a result of an exchange arrangement through which Cary Grant came to Warner Bros. to star in *Arsenic and Old Lace*. *Sahara* was a conventional war film, derived in part from a Russian film. The scriptwriter, as for *Action in the North Atlantic*, was John Howard Lawson who was later to become one of the Hollywood Ten accused of putting Communist propaganda on the screen, but *Sahara* owes more to *The Lost Patrol* and others of that ilk than to any Russian influence.

Bogart was Joe Gunn, the sergeant commanding a tank called Lulubelle in the Libyan desert after the fall of Tobruk. In the general retreat, he and his two crew take on a number of passengers, forming the usual international cross-section – English, French, Sudanese, South African and Irish allies, plus German and Italian prisoners. The main quest is to find water. They reach a waterhole just ahead of a huge contingent of thirsty Germans and decide to defend it. Eventually, Bogart is one of only two survivors and he shouts final defiance at the Germans as they surge forward in a huge wave, only to find they are intent on surrendering to him.

Sahara communicates a powerful sense of the harsh, arid desert terrain through Rudolph Maté's bleached, dusty images. As in Bogart's previous film, characterisation is a poor second to spectacle. Bogart's character is a decent, average guy whose home is the army. In a film espousing group effort, it was only right that he should not stand out, though he was the sole star name in the cast. However, in his address to the men, persuading them to stay and fight the Germans, his performance does strike a distinctive note through the controlled intensity of his argument.

Back at Warner Bros., Bogart made a cameo appearance along with a dozen other top stars in the musical comedy extravaganza *Thank Your Lucky Stars*. He arrives unshaven at the back of a theatre, demanding to see the star, Eddie Cantor. His aggressive behaviour upsets S.Z. 'Cuddles' Sakall, and, ticked off by the tubby character actor who tells him emphatically that he is not wanted in Cantor's show, Bogart backs away, scratching his neck and murmuring, 'Gee, I hope none of my movie fans hear about this.'

Bogart was looking forward to making *Passage to Marseille*, a film specially devised to consolidate his success in *Casablanca*, but he was ordered to fit in a thriller before that, called *Conflict*, in which he would play, of all things, a wife murderer.

Phoning studio casting boss Steve Trilling on 6 May, with shooting scheduled to start on the following Monday, he found himself instead in a long, repetitive conversation with Jack L. Warner. Bogart asked, as a favour, to be taken off the film, declaring, 'Nothing you can say will convince me it is a good picture, or is in good shape, or for me.' Warner was totally unyielding and tried several tacks to persuade Bogart to report for filming, claiming that he had personally bought it for Bogart, that it would be an important picture and that Bogart would be suspended if he didn't play in it and would lose *Passage to Marseille*. 'Please understand that I am not threatening you. I don't threaten anyone,' said Warner at one point. Clearly, the studio boss was only concerned that the picture shouldn't be delayed, but one sympathises with Bogart as he struggles to remain civil and gets nowhere. It is a little chilling to find that Warner had the entire conversation recorded and typed-up (the transcript appears in Rudy Behlmer's fascinating collection of studio documents, *Inside Warner Bros.*). At the end of the discussion, Bogart refused to do the film; yet later he decided to make it.

In fact, after *Conflict* was completed, it was shelved along with several other Warner pictures of the period including *Saratoga Trunk* and *Arsenic and Old Lace* to make way for films which were more topical.

Bogart went straight into *Passage to Marseille*, after completing *Conflict* in August 1943. The film represented some wishful thinking on Warner Bros.' part. They seemed to believe that putting most of the stars and the director of *Casablanca* to work on a shallow script might somehow result in a film with the same popular appeal. Though Michael Curtiz and cameraman James Wong Howe invest the film with striking, moody images, the script's complicated structure and rudimentary characterisation prevent it from meaning much. Bogart plays a crusading French journalist, Jean Matrac (he wisely attempts no accent), who opposes appeasement at Munich in 1938; his hatred of Fascism leads to his incarceration on Devil's Island on a trumped-up murder charge. He escapes with other convicts and alone remains silent while they affirm their patriotism and promise to fight for their country in the war against Germany.

Bogart portrays Matrac as a frighteningly intense and humourless figure. His romance with Michèle Morgan's Paula is perfunctorily developed and interrupted by political events. Their affair does not have the impact of the Paris scenes in *Casablanca*. Matrac's disillusionment with his country while on Devil's Island is vividly etched in scenes of him striding up and down his cell, railing against the injustice that has brought him there. He coldbloodedly murders a prisoner who tries to horn in on their escape. On board the freighter, he tells Captain Freycinet (Claude Rains) that he has no intention of fighting for France and only intends returning to Paula, who becomes his wife.

But when Major Duval (Sydney Greenstreet) takes over the ship, the twitch in Bogart's right cheek, the only movement in his otherwise grim face, forebodes trouble for the Fascist sympathiser. Bogart helps overthrow Duval and guns down the German plane that attacks the ship, wounding both the mess boy and one of his fellow escaped convincts (Peter Lorre). When Bogart spots survivors from the crashed plane drifting in the water, he rushes along the deck to a machine-gun and fires on them. Bogart's subsequent death from wounds received as a gunner on a bombing raid over Germany is a delayed form of retribution.

Because of Matrac's fanaticism he is not an admirable character. He needs to commit himself totally to a cause, as he did in politics before the war. Even his last letter to his son, read at a bleakly shot cliff-top funeral, is more an outlet for his fervent beliefs than the feelings of a loving father. Thus Matrac hints at other dark figures to come in the gallery of Bogart's characters whose deep-seated emotions get the better of them.

Michèle Morgan had much the same experience as Ingrid Bergman did when working with Bogart. In a 1974 *Radio Times* interview, she recalled, 'Bogart was a strange man ... he was nice to me, but not over-nice. I was very young and shy, and he was at the height of his career. He was approaching his divorce from his first [sic] wife, and they quarrelled all the time – that didn't affect his acting but it seemed to make him very reserved. I don't recall ever having had a long conversation with him, and if you were to ask me what my strongest impression of him was – well, I think I should say, a man who was always on his guard.'

But Billy Roy, who played the small but important role of the mess boy, recalled Bogart as an actor who went out of his way to help the inexperienced youth after Michael Curtiz gave him a hard time. James Wong Howe also remembered working with Bogart: 'He was drinking heavily at the time. He and Mayo Methot fought continually, marvellous great rows that would always take place in other people's houses, which would finish up with Methot doing something like throwing all her jewellery in Bogart's face and walking out, after which he would spend the rest of the night drinking. Somehow he always managed to be at the studio the next day, and even if he'd been up all night, he could turn in a good performance. In fact, my most vivid memory of him at that time wasn't on set; it was the sight of him coming down a road early one morning. He was hung-over and dishevelled and he was on his way to ask me if I could stall things for him at the studios: "If you can get them to hang on for half an hour, Jimmy," he said, "I'll be there." I must have looked a bit doubtful, because he said, "Don't worry, I'll be OK." And, of course, he was.'

Executive producer Hal Wallis described the Bogart of this period: 'The moment the day's work was over, he drove home, and seldom mingled with the other players ... [His and Mayo's] fights were legendary ...'

Bogart's aloofness with his leading ladies was partly designed to avoid giving Mayo grounds for jealousy. He defended his wife's behaviour as best he could. 'She's an actress,' he said, 'a damned good one, but she's not working much at the moment – which is tough for her. Understand?' In fact, she made her last screen appearance in Warners' *Brother Rat and a Baby* (1940), and seems to have considered further small parts (which Bogart could have persuaded Warners to provide) as beneath her dignity.

Early in December 1943, Louise Brooks remembers seeing Bogart and Mayo at the 21 Club in New York. 'I was shocked to see how dreadfully Humphrey's face had aged. The effects of the war he had waged against his inertia – work and whiskey without sleep and food – were visible at last. Mayo looked as though she had just got out of bed with her clothes on. Her suit was rumpled, her hair not combed, her face not made up. They sat at a table in the far corner of the room as if they wanted to be alone, yet they neither spoke nor looked at each other till their drinks were brought to the table. Then Mayo turned to speak fiercely to Humphrey, as if she were continuing some argument that could never be resolved. Slumped against the banquette, unmoved, he stared at his hand slowly turning the glass round and round. It was plain that the team of "The Battling Bogarts" was soon to break up.'

They were on their way to Italy and North Africa to entertain the troops and chat with wounded servicemen. Films and visits from movie stars were regarded as the most important morale boosters after food and letters from home. After arriving in North

Africa on 11 December, Bogart met up with John Huston, who was making a documentary, and they decided that they would try to fly over the front. After Bogart used his influence to obtain a Piper plane, Huston discovered that it would be much too dangerous to fly such a slow-moving aircraft in range of the enemy's guns and the idea was scrapped. Yet there were high jinks, as Huston later recalled – the Bogarts swore at a general in Naples who objected to the noise from a party they were giving for enlisted men in their hotel room, and they were very quickly moved to another zone.

'In Italy we played most shows within three or four miles from the front,' the actor said on returning to Hollywood in February. 'There we found soldiers seeing 16mm films during brief rest periods from active fighting. Every special service officer we talked to stressed the vital function motion pictures play in maintaining morale. They also stressed the importance of men in forward areas getting the best and latest pictures.' In fact, the Hollywood studios supplied copies of their new pictures for service shows as soon as they were ready, usually before they were released to theatres back home.

Bogart went into Warner Bros. on Monday 21 February, for work on a short, *Report from the Front*, which displayed previously unshown combat footage along with scenes of his recent visit. Bogart narrated the three-minute film which preceded the year's collection from movie-theatre audiences for the Red Cross. Besides his voluntary trip overseas, Bogart, who had been a junior commander in spare-time service with the Coastguard before the war, made a regular contribution to the war effort in the Coastguard Reserve, taking his launch *Sluggy* (named after Mayo) out at nights on anti-submarine patrol along the Californian coastline.

9

BOGART MEETS BACALL

To Have and Have Not paired Bogart, then in his mid-forties, with a newcomer named Lauren Bacall, then aged nineteen. She had been spotted on a magazine cover by director Howard Hawks, who had signed her to a personal contract and carefully trained her to speak with a low voice. She had first met Bogart on a visit to the set of *Passage to Marseille*, unaware that she would be his leading lady in his next picture. It was not love at first sight, but they were attracted to each other after shooting began on *To Have and Have Not* in March 1944. As Howard Hawks recalled (in Joseph McBride's *Hawks on Hawks*): 'When two people are falling in love with each other, they're not tough to get along with, I can tell you that. Bogie was marvellous. I said, "You've got to help," and, of course, after a few days he really began to get interested in the girl. That made him help more. And it wasn't hard at all. She found out that people liked her and that it didn't hurt her. She just waltzed through that picture … And the funny thing is that Bogie fell in love with the character she played, so she had to keep playing it the rest of her life.'

This was the final stage in the remarkable evolution of Bogart's image from the days when he was a sour-faced heavy. Their scenes together were electric. Today, they retain an impact but their effect is as much comic as sensual. Hawks realised the only way to make sense of the disparity in their ages was to have the girl dominate Bogart and to have Bogart allow it because he enjoys her extravagant performance. Hawks gave her 'a quality of insolence' that was reminiscent of Dietrich and seemed original in a young American woman. Bacall has related an instance when Bogart helped her performance: recalling an old love scene of Lunt and Fontanne on stage, he suggested she should run her hand up the side of his face after they've kissed and give him a playful slap before saying 'Why don't you shave and we'll try it again?'

The plot was a superficial reworking of the situations in *Casablanca*, with aspects of the Ernest Hemingway novel (which gave the film its title) tacked on. Here was Bogart as Harry Morgan, an adventurer who runs a boat in French territory, Martinique, which hopes to remain neutral after the fall of France. In *Casablanca*, he parried Conrad Veidt's question about his nationality by calling himself a drunkard; here he responds to equally tiresome and unnecessary probing by declaring himself an Eskimo before becoming more co-operative. Here he declines to become involved in what he calls 'local politics' just as he ignored the underground in *Casablanca*. 'What are your sympathies?' he is asked. 'Minding my own business,' he replies. In *Casablanca* the Prefect of Police suggested Bogart helped the resistance leader because of his dislike for Veidt's Nazi, and here Bogart gives a similar explanation for finally undertaking a hazardous trip for the Resistance: 'Maybe because I like you and I don't like them.'

In characteristic Hawks manner, broad issues are not as important as personal relationships. Bogart's character first works for the Resistance not from conviction but to buy a plane ticket to dispatch Slim (Lauren Bacall) to safety. He keeps Walter Brennan's 'rummy', Eddie, on the payroll because he was once a good man. He is encouraging towards the tourist who hires his boat for fishing, until the man proves exasperating and unworthy. The Vichy police chief (Dan Seymour) rapidly angers him by his behaviour – his rough questioning of Bacall prompts Bogart to step forward – 'Go ahead, slap me!' he challenges one of the chief's men. Then, when the chief gets rough with Walter Brennan, Bogart really explodes, turning the tables on Seymour, pistol-whipping him into arranging Brennan's release over the telephone. But such scenes are eclipsed by the love scenes made famous by such lines as 'If you want me, just whistle.' In actual fact that line is a little more complicated. It follows Bacall kissing Bogart and remarking, 'It's even better when you help,' then declaring, 'You know you don't have to act with me, Steve. You don't have to say anything and you don't have to do anything. Not a thing. Oh, maybe just whistle. You know how to whistle, don't you, Steve? You just put your lips together – and blow.' As she leaves him, Bogart experimentally puts his lips together, lets out a low whistle, and smiles to himself. Bacall is aware that Bogart has been badly burnt by a woman, and their scenes are loaded with fire symbolism: lighting matches, smoking cigarettes, exhaling smoke.

Bogart had reluctantly given up his leading ladies at the end of *The Maltese Falcon* and *Casablanca*, but here he got to keep Bacall – and eventually in real life, too. First, Bogart tried to patch up his marriage but Mayo Methot's drinking and bad temper continued. He announced a trial separation but went back to her after she became ill and was hospitalised. He was afraid of what she might do to herself, having seen one of his sisters die young, apparently through alcoholism, and the other confined to a sanitarium.

Even before *To Have and Have Not* went into release (it became a box-office smash in January 1945), Hawks had teamed him with Bacall in another film, *The Big Sleep*. It began shooting on 10 October 1944, and the strain of working during the day with Bacall while worrying about Mayo began to tell. On the day after Christmas, a normal working day, Bogart didn't turn up and was found drunk and asleep at his wife's house. The film's unit manager, Eric Stacey, informed the studio: 'I really do not feel that Bogart's condition can be straightened out overnight since he has been drinking for approximately three weeks and it is not only the liquor, but also the mental turmoil regarding his domestic life that is entering into this situation ...' Stacey added that Bogart had almost always arrived at the set on time over the previous ten weeks of shooting but that Hawks had often been dissatisfied with his performance, and had to stop work to have long discussions with him.

Shooting was completed on 13 January 1945, having over-run the forty-two-day schedule by thirty-four days, not only because of the problems with Bogart but also because Hawks was rewriting the script all the time (though, in one case, he cut out scenes and saved so much time that the film didn't go over budget by much).

Bogart moved out of his home into the Garden of Allah and persuaded Mayo that their marriage was over. He revealed his new romantic attachment to Bacall to a columnist in February and it became national news, whipped up for all it was worth by studio publicists. Mayo went to Reno and eventually stayed for the six weeks necessary to qualify for the divorce. John Huston wrote in *An Open Book*: 'She was forever "on stage" – raucous and demanding. Bogie indulged her and did his best to placate her. But let her feel attention shifting away from her person and there would be hell to pay. She was known to throw plates in restaurants and wield knives. I can only marvel at Bogie's putting up with her as long as he did.' (She left Hollywood and died in Portland, Oregon, on 9 June 1951, aged only 47, apparently as a result of acute alcoholism. Whereas Bogart remained on friendly terms with his earlier wives and saw them occasionally, this wasn't possible with Mayo.)

On 21 May 1945, eleven days after the divorce became final, he married Bacall. The wedding took place on the Ohio farm of Bogart's friend, the author Louis Bromfield (one of those novels was the basis of the actor's 1940 film, *It All Came True*). 'Bogie shed tears all through the ceremony,' the new Mrs. Bogart later recalled, adding: 'He always cries at weddings.' There was little time for a honeymoon as Bogart had interrupted the shooting of his current picture, *The Two Mrs. Carrolls*, while Bacall had to start a new movie, *Confidential Agent*, with Charles Boyer. (In a curious switch, Bogart had been announced to star in the film in December 1944, but with Eleanor Parker as his co-star, not Bacall.)

The Big Sleep was one of many films made available for showing to servicemen before anyone else. It was more than a year after the headline marriage before ordinary theatre audiences were able to see the Bogarts together in the film.

Instead, *Conflict* made its much delayed appearance. Though shot, of course, long before Bogart had ever met Bacall, the film does curiously foreshadow the major change in his life with its story of a man disposing of his wife (Rose Hobart), because he loves a younger woman (in this case, his wife's sister, played by Alexis Smith). But his Richard Mason is not allowed to reap any happiness from the murder: Alexis Smith does not fall into his arms, and he inadvertently reveals his guilt to a psychologist (Sydney Greenstreet). The latter contrives a thoroughly far-fetched scheme to worry Bogart's character. He ensures that the man returns to the scene of the crime by making him think his wife is still alive, where he is arrested by the police.

The part benefitted from Bogart's ability to convey nervous agitation. The way in which he frightens the landlady of an empty apartment into which a woman resembling his wife has vanished, or tries to bully Alexis Smith into loving him, anticipates the murderous rages and desperate needs of his Dixon Steele in *In a Lonely Place*.

Though Bogart is highly effective, the film was a minor melodrama that didn't deserve his presence. He had been right to argue and plead with Jack Warner, and subsequent developments now made it even more unsuitable. For this did absolutely nothing to strengthen his newly-found romantic and heroic image, which was as much an asset to the studio as to himself. In fact, it did positive harm.

Warners had another huge, self-inflicted problem: the setback to Lauren Bacall's budding career caused by miscasting her as a humourless aristocratic English girl in *Confidential Agent*. It had been rushed out because of its topical subject matter, and her performance had been savaged by the critics. It was vital that she recovered the impact she made in her first film. The studio couldn't afford to miss with *The Big Sleep*.

Shortly before its release, movie-goers were teased by a brief appearance of the Bogarts in a comedy called *Two Guys from Milwaukee* starring Dennis Morgan and Jack Carson. Lauren Bacall is the dream girl of Morgan's Balkan prince turned beer salesman, but his good fortune in finding himself next to her on a plane is dashed by a tap on the shoulder from a tough-acting Bogart who demands his seat.

When *The Big Sleep* finally appeared, it contained some sultry new footage which the armed forces had never seen as it was shot by Hawks early in 1946 to add more sparkle to the scenes between Bogart and Bacall. The director claimed the work prevented him watching some of his horses run at Santa Anita racetrack which gave him the idea for a provocative new scene of sexual flirtation in which copulation is compared with a jockey handling a horse, in a series of double entendres so sophisticated that the Hays Office allowed them through.

In *The Big Sleep*, Bogart portrayed Raymond Chandler's tough private eye, Philip Marlowe, in an intrigue so labyrinthine that it made *The Maltese Falcon* look like a nursery rhyme. He uncovers a plot involving gambling, pornography, blackmail and murder, and during his travels encounters a bevy of beautiful women: even his taxi-driver is female and willing, while a prim-looking woman (Dorothy Malone) closes her bookshop early and lets down her hair to spend an hour over a bottle of rye with him. The only woman who takes a dim view of his antics is Agnes (Sonia Darrin), but he does antagonise her with his masquerade in the antiquarian bookshop: a pair of spectacles rests on the end of his nose, his hat brim is turned up, his voice lisping and effeminate. Though suggested in Chandler's novel, Hawks has credited Bogart with developing these characteristics when asked to liven up the scene.

Much of the film is devoted to slick banter – Bacall's first words to Marlowe are: 'My, you're a mess, aren't you!' Bogart responds: 'I'm not very tall either. Next time I'll come on stilts.' Bacall's character is an enigmatic figure, clearly involved in a cover-up, as apt to mention Marcel Proust as display a provocative leg, but mainly a woman who enjoys tomfoolery like teasing a police sergeant over the telephone with Bogart's help.

Bogart also trades smart answers with such figures as Eddie Mars (John Ridgely) who threatens to make Bogart's business his business. 'You wouldn't like it,' Bogart tells him. 'The pay's too small.' But eventually the fun stops as Bogart stubbornly refuses to be paid off and gives a classic justification: 'Too many people told me to stop.' He encounters in Bob Steele's Canino one of the meanest adversaries ever to inhabit the screen: Canino poisons a doughty private eye (another of Elisha Cook Jr.'s unfortunate losers), and is taken very seriously indeed by Bogart who describes him as the kind of man who'd knock all your teeth out and then punch you in the stomach for mumbling. In their final confrontation, Bogart dispenses with the usual screen formality of allowing the other side to get off the first shot and shoots Canino before he can fire. Bogart's showdown with John Ridgely is presented as another gruelling experience, and *The Big Sleep* is doubly satisfactory because of it – a fun picture that is also a tense thriller.

After Bogart finished *The Two Mrs. Carrolls* in July 1945, it was shelved for nearly two years. There were plans in October for Lauren Bacall and him to make a film called *The Devil Was A Lady* for producer Robert Buckner and director Raoul Walsh, but the plans fell through. Then Bogart was to take the title role in something called *The Dealer's Name Is George*, which would have been yet another hand-me-down from George Raft had it been made (Raft had refused it in 1942). A bizarre project, announced in February 1946, was for Bogart to star in *The Life of Jack Benny*, from a screenplay by William Morrow for producer Jerry Wald. This was to have been a tongue-in-cheek fantasy in which Bogart re-enacted famous Benny sketches.

Then Warners decided that Bogart and Bacall should make *Stallion Road*, a romantic drama with a horse ranching background that would also co-star Ronald Reagan. In the story, Reagan's character would win the girl rather than Bogart's. The Bogarts refused to make the picture and were put on suspension without salary while Zachary Scott and Alexis Smith were rushed in to appear with Reagan.

Jack Warner then agreed to a new contract under which Bogart would make only one picture a year for Warner Bros. for the fee of $200,000, could reject two out of three properties, and had director approval.

The contract was to run for fifteen years.

All this kept Bogart from making a new film for almost a year, although he did dub his voice in an Errol Flynn comedy, *Never Say Goodbye*, to help Flynn carry off a perfect Bogie imitation. His return to work was on a loan-out to Columbia for *Dead Reckoning* while details were finalised on his new Warner contract. Warners gave Columbia Bogart to pay back studio boss Harry Cohn for stars he had earlier loaned them.

Cohn wanted his top female star, Rita Hayworth, to play opposite Bogart in *Dead Reckoning*, but they were feuding over her contract and Bogart refused to accept Marguerite Chapman or Evelyn Keyes in her place. Cohn went after Lauren Bacall but she was under suspension and Jack Warner refused to lift it. Lizabeth Scott had to be borrowed from Hal Wallis's new independent company at Paramount. To direct the film, Bogart accepted an old friend from the start of his acting career, John Cromwell. *Dead Reckoning* went hurriedly into production, in June 1946.

As Rip Murdock, former paratrooper and war hero, Bogart lands in hot water investigating the disappearance of his best pal in Gulf City, Florida. A hopelessly contrived plot and dreary dialogue are further handicapped by weak casting of cops and villains (Columbia just didn't have Warners' wealth in supporting players), while the musical score is particularly ineffective. A scripting absurdity requires Bogart to knowingly swallow a drugged drink rather than betray the bartender who tips him off about it (and yet Bogart wakes up to find the barman's corpse alongside him).

This is a violent film with post-war trimmings – Bogart takes it and he dishes it out, terrorising his opponents with an incendiary device that's a combat souvenir – but the main interest lies in the pairing of Bogart with the husky-voiced twenty-three-year-old blonde, Lizabeth Scott. A hot new discovery – a

variation on Veronica Lake, but even more a sultry
rival to Bacall – she was tougher and more hard-boiled
than both and was publicised as 'The Threat'. This was
her third film and her first major role. Cast as a
nightclub singer from the wrong side of the tracks, she
is an assured partner for Bogart, especially in the
clinches, but her role never makes a great deal of
sense. Betrayed by a whiff of jasmine as she blackjacks
Bogart, she ends up trying to shoot him. He
compliments her on being 'awfully good' as a deceiver
and likens her further to a Brigid O'Shaughnessy with
his reasons for turning her in ('a guy's pal's killed, he
ought to do something about it,' etc.). Perhaps Bogart
himself worked in these variations on *The Maltese
Falcon*'s dialogue in an effort to improve the scenes,
though his delivery lacks the same intensity of feeling.

Bogart might have contributed the misogynous lines
about how the ideal woman would come capsule-size,
to be carried round in the pocket and enlarged with
the wave of a wand when necessary, a suggestion that
the Lizabeth Scott character understandably finds
outrageous. Just to be provocative in interviews and
party gatherings, the actor made a habit of arguing the
case for such pocket-size dames who could be put away
when they talked too much.

Despite its fairly high standing as a Bogart picture
and *film noir*, *Dead Reckoning* is distinctly second-rate. It
made no great stir at the box-office and was less
popular than *The Two Mrs. Carrolls* which finally went
into release after it in spring 1947.

The Two Mrs. Carrolls cast him opposite Barbara
Stanwyck in his most lunatic role since *The Return of
Doctor X*. As a wife murderer in *Conflict* he'd been fairly
sane and had a conventional motive; in this film he was
a painter, Geoffrey Carroll, who kills old wives and
marries new ones to get the creative juices flowing
again. As always, Bogart gave a sharply delineated

performance, but he was at the mercy of director Peter Godfrey's demands. He uses his characteristic expression of rage in his attic workplace, tapping his brush, flinging down his cigarette and wiping the canvas clean of unsatisfactory work. But he is periodically required to finger his right temple as a sign of mental disarray, and when his daughter mentions that Van Gogh was insane, he stiffens, seizes the book she is reading, and feverishly strokes his temple again. When Bogart finds wife number two (Barbara Stanwyck) has thrown away her poisoned milk and rumbled his intentions, he feels both temples. Soon after, he makes a rainsoaked appearance at her bedroom window, his arms stretched out to thrust the curtains apart, looking like a gleeful vampire on a nocturnal call.

Even worse is the way Godfrey telegraphs Bogart's madness with sinisterly lit, eye-bulging, and face-quivering close-ups. The director also lays on the atmosphere of a leafy English cathedral town far too heavily, and oversees a dreadful mismatch while Bogart is strangling Stanwyck on her bed: in one shot, his face is trembling with the effort but in a close-up it is perfectly still. Godfrey never even makes Alexis Smith enough of an inspiration to warrant Bogart doing away with Stanwyck.

Bogart's last appearance in the film, being led away by the police, carries a frank admission of the absurdity of it all, as he is allowed to turn and ask his two escorts, 'Would you gentlemen like a drink? A glass of milk, perhaps?' Warners, who also encouraged Peter Godfrey to play around with Errol Flynn's image in *Cry Wolf* (1947), had a big investment to recover since *The Two Mrs. Carrolls* had been a hit play, but it seems a most curious use of Bogart (character actor Victor Jory played Geoffrey Carroll on Broadway). Clearly part of the eighteen months' delay in releasing the film was to space it away from Bogart's uxoricidal endeavours in

Conflict, but some of it must have been corporate embarrassment at the way the film had turned out.

Back in January 1945, it had been announced that Bogart was to play Sime Silverman, the founder of the trade paper *Variety*, in *Mr. Broadway*, based on a biography by Abel Green. This would have seemed odd if several other equally improbable players, including John Garfield and Cary Grant, hadn't also been mentioned for the part. (As the general public didn't know what Silverman looked like, to Hollywood thinking it didn't matter who played him.) A year later, while writer Richard Brooks was working on this project, producer Jerry Wald briefly considered Spencer Tracy for the role. Brooks turned in his script in May 1946 and *Mr. Broadway* was scheduled to start in September with Bogart once again the most likely star. But it was never made and in November Bogart began a much more suitable assignment at Warners.

Partly shot on San Francisco locations, *Dark Passage* is worthy of better recognition than it generally enjoys. It is certainly the most tender of the Bogart/Bacall films, and a beguiling and offbeat romantic drama. Superficially, Bogart is completely wrong for his part as Vincent Parry, a convicted wife-murderer (this time innocent). He breaks out of San Quentin and tries to become master of his fate, but finds himself utterly dependent on other people. He especially relies on Lauren Bacall's character, a wealthy artist who has convinced herself of his innocence and remains true to him even when he seems responsible for two further deaths. For her, helping Bogart is a way of getting even with society for her father's fate (he died in prison, also convicted of murdering his wife) and Bogart is a substitute father figure on whom to lavish her concern. Her need for him is reciprocated: Bogart is grateful as well as attracted to the artist, and this is the basis for their successful relationship.

In this film, the familiar Bogart face is a disguise created by a plastic surgeon. Making innovative use of a lightweight camera devised by the Nazis, writer/director Delmer Daves ingeniously went in for a great deal of subjective camerawork to avoid showing Bogart before he looks like Bogart. At first, we hear the familiar voice but see a different face in the newspapers so that we know that Parry doesn't look like Bogart. In fact, this face is a composite of Bogart's eyes and eyebrows, which would have been unaltered in plastic surgery, and the features of Bogart's stunt double. It is more than an hour into the film before the bandages come off and Bogart's character peers at his unshaven features, curious to see what he now looks like.

The film is about faith (Bogart's) and charity (that of others). Bogart has a moment of doubt as the surgeon fingers his razor and contemplates the range of possibilities open to him; his eyes signal alarm as Lauren Bacall seems to be betraying him; and he has his real enemies. The old Bogart persona emerges in his handling of a blackmailer after he is forced into action, but when he confronts Agnes Moorehead's character, the real killer of his wife, and tries to make her confess, he begs as much as he harasses her. In her venomous behaviour, Moorehead is the complete opposite of Bacall (just as the two men that drive Bogart – cabbie and crook – are total contrasts): Bacall stakes her own freedom on helping Bogart while Moorehead flings herself to her death rather than clear his name. Her fall is oddly described by Bogart as an accident though it looks deliberate and makes most sense as a last cruel jest on her part. In the final scene, Bogart is reunited with Bacall in a sunny Peruvian paradise, an unexpectedly blissful answer to his unsolved problem.

Immediately after finishing the picture, Bogart agreed to help the Palestinian cause by flying to

Chicago and donating his services to the touring production of Ben Hecht's pageant *A Flag Is Born*, which had starred Paul Muni and, later, Luther Adler. (Bogart himself was a gentile; Lauren Bacall was Jewish, though non-practising.) The poorly-reviewed production was a fund raiser by the American League for a Free Palestine to help homeless European Jews reach Israel, and Bogart took over the narrator's role from his friend Louis Bromfield who had begun the four-week run at the Studebaker Theatre in January 1947 (the original Broadway narrator had been Quentin Reynolds, later succeeded by Ruth Chatterton and Alexander Scourby). It seems to have been the only time Bogart returned to the stage after his success in *The Petrified Forest*.

10

OF GOLD AND POLITICS

If Bogart's work in *Dark Passage* is not always given its
due, his powerful performance as Fred C. Dobbs, the
gold prospector of John Huston's *The Treasure of the
Sierra Madre*, has been well recognised. In 1941, flushed
with his success in *The Maltese Falcon*, the director had
persuaded Jack Warner to seek the film rights to
B. Traven's acclaimed novel, but by the time all the
complications of dealing with the reclusive and enigmatic author had been surmounted, Huston was on wartime service and the film was postponed until he was
able to write the screenplay in 1946.

Jack Warner was persuaded to allow most of the
filming to be done in Mexico, making it one of the first
Hollywood pictures essentially shot abroad. Bogart,
who had no interest in travel, was required to perform
on foreign soil for the first time, apart from his troop
shows in Italy and North Africa. Production started in
March 1947 at Tampico, then moved to the mountains
west of Mexico City, near San José de Perua (but night
scenes were done on the sound stages back at
Burbank). Shooting in Mexico extended way beyond
schedule and Bogart became worried that he might not
be able to get away in time to run his fifty-four- (or
fifty-five-) foot, sixteen-ton ocean-class yacht called the
Santana, which was his pride and joy, in the annual
Fourth-of-July race to Honolulu. After winning many
cups with his earlier sailboats, Bogart had bought the
racing yawl in December 1945 from Dick Powell and

June Allyson (Ray Milland had also used it for a while).
Perhaps in imitation of Errol Flynn's yacht which was
called the *Sirocco*, it took its name from a hot, dry wind
that blew off the mountains of Southern California
and was called the Santa Anna, or 'Santana' by the
Indians.

Bogart's anxiety to get back to his sailboat
temporarily soured his relationship with Huston, who
naturally put his precious movie before anything else.
Finally, Huston became so annoyed at Bogart's
nagging over his slowness that the director reached out
and twisted his nose until the tears flowed. Bogart quit
complaining and missed the race as shooting dragged
on to 22 July.

Despite its reputation as a more serious film,
The Treasure of the Sierra Madre is far less compelling as a
psychological study of the effects of greed than *The
Maltese Falcon*: the falcon was 'the stuff that dreams are
made of', enough to cause men to kill one another; in
this film it is gold, and the point is hammered home
rather than allowed to emerge. *Treasure* is too long, too
linear in development, too unvaried in tone; it is a film
to be respected more than enjoyed, especially when
Walter Huston's worldly-wise old-timer hints at what
will happen – he says discovering gold can change a
man's soul, and even caused him to murder a partner –
though the ingenuous Bogart scoffs perhaps a little bit
too heartily.

But the film's performances are extraordinary:
Walter Huston was deservedly nominated for an Oscar
and won, and Bogart, in a startling study of moral
disintegration, is at least as impressive, though he was
ignored by the Academy on this occasion. In a really
brave departure from his leading man image, Bogart
demonstrated his loyalty to Huston and his willingness
to sacrifice his image for the sake of a meaty,
challenging part, to show the range he had as an actor.
Jack Warner was horrified to learn that his star ended

up being killed by bandits and, though his beheading by machete was made less brutal following adverse reaction at a sneak preview, Bogart successfully supported Huston in his bid to resist further studio interference.

Bogart's Fred C. Dobbs begins the film as a likeable scrounger, cadging handouts from fellow Americans in Tampico, Mexico, and glad to have the opportunity of working on a construction job with a fellow down-and-out (Tim Holt). When the contractor (Barton MacLane), cheats them out of their wages, they catch up with him and Bogart beats him up, but he is careful to relieve him only of what they are owed and to pay for the damage they've caused to the bar-room. This honest act emphasises that at the outset Bogart is a basically decent fellow with strength of character – though later not enough to withstand the corrosive effect of gold. 'He was as honest as the next fellow,' comments Walter Huston at the end of the film, but the bar-room incident shows that he is a little more honest than most.

Bogart's character's fertile imagination and greenhorn's eagerness are his undoing. He is the first to tire on the journey, though he earlier doubts the old man's ability to keep up with them and he loses his temper with the old man at the very moment the veteran gold-seeker has detected a promising site to excavate. Bogart scoffs at the idea of each man hiding his share of the gold they've found: 'What a dirty, filthy mind you've got,' he tells Huston, adding, 'Only a thief at heart would think of an idea like that!' All three of the men show signs of moral disintegration, and are prepared to kill the interloper (Bruce Bennett), but it is Bogart who succumbs to a paranoid suspicion of the other two. His mind finds treachery in every suggestion they make, leading ultimately to his attempt to murder Tim Holt's character, persuading himself that he'll be murdered if he doesn't. The part gave

Bogart scope to explore the irritable, nervous side of his character as when, convinced that his partner is dead, he is racked by indecision about whether to bury or leave the body. Only the chilling arrival of the bandits as he lies defenceless at the water hole concentrates his fevered mind; desperately he tries to negotiate an escape from their clutches but in vain. The film should end when Bogart dies, and the gold is dispatched to the wind by the bandits, who are ignorant of its worth, but instead the film's message is hammered home in words from the two survivors.

John Huston later won Academy Awards for writing and directing the film. Immediately after finishing it, he agreed to co-write (with Richard Brooks) and direct a more commercial picture that would team him again with Bogart: *Key Largo*. Bogart was also one of many Warner stars who made cameo appearances in a minor comedy, *Always Together*, starring Robert Hutton and Joyce Reynolds – he was seen in a parody of *Stella Dallas* as a tearful outcast of a father, pressing his face against a rainswept windowpane.

Bogart had long been a liberal in his political outlook. He had campaigned for Roosevelt's re-election in the 1944 presidential campaign at a time when it was considered advisable for actors to keep their political views private rather than alienate any of their fans. Many listeners objected when he broadcast his support for F.D.R. over the radio in November 1944. The actor vigorously defended his right to express a political opinion in an article for the *Saturday Evening Post* (10 February 1945), entitled 'I Stuck My Neck Out', and he vowed to speak his mind in future. (Wife Mayo had actively supported the rival candidate which had given them something more to battle over.)

In 1947, it was time for Bogart to stick his neck out again. The members of the House Un-American Activities Committee, who were led by J. Parnell

Thomas, and included Richard Nixon, were hunting Communists in the film industry and seeking fame and attention for themselves. Most of Hollywood was opposed to the Congressional Committee's investigations which amounted to a witch-hunt; but many, including Jack Warner, testified in preliminary interviews, naming writers and others who might be Communists.

John Huston, William Wyler and screenwriter Philip Dunne formed the Committee for the First Amendment – the Amendment that guaranteed freedom of speech and political belief. They were joined by Bogart, Lauren Bacall and many other leading figures who supported its case that '... any investigation into the political beliefs of the individual is contrary to the basic principles of our democracy. Any attempt to curb freedom of expression and to set arbitrary standards of Americanism is in itself disloyal to both the spirit and letter of the Constitution.'

When HUAC issued subpoenas forcing various writers and others, some of whom would become known as 'the Hollywood Ten', to appear before it in Washington, members of the First Amendment Committee gathered at Edward G. Robinson's house for a discussion with the men who had been called. The Bogarts attended, along with Katharine Hepburn, John Garfield and others. It was decided that as many of the Committee who could would fly to Washington to present a petition to the House of Representatives outlining the abuses of HUAC's methods, and to support industry spokesman Eric Johnston. Besides the Bogarts, those who made the trip in October included Huston and his actress wife Evelyn Keyes, Larry Adler, Richard Conte, Ira Gershwin, Sterling Hayden, June Havoc, Paul Henreid, Gene Kelly, Danny Kaye, Marsha Hunt and Jane Wyatt. But it was Bogart, as the most celebrated member of the group, whom the press picked out as the leader.

What Huston and others wanted was for the subpoenaed men to declare their political beliefs in public and then to refuse to testify before HUAC. But the men declined the first step and not without reason: they were entitled to keep their beliefs private and an admission that they were or had been Communists would have destroyed their careers. On Monday 27 October, the Hollywood delegation took their seats at the hearings and Chairman Thomas called writer John Howard Lawson to the stand. He knew that Lawson would be a hostile witness and it would appear that the celebrities had come to support him rather than their highly respected industry representative, Eric Johnston. Lawson gave an insolent and provocative performance as did two further witnesses, which inwardly dismayed Bogart and colleagues. But Bogart spoke out: 'We sat in the Committee room and heard it happen. We saw the gavel of the Committee Chairman cutting off the words of free Americans. The sound of that gavel, Mr. Thomas, rings across America, and every time your gavel struck, it hit the First Amendment of the Constitution of the United States.' The words are so effective that one wonders if they were drafted for Bogart by Huston or Dunne; they certainly gained tremendous power from Bogart's measured and resonant delivery.

It quickly became apparent that the unfriendly witnesses had turned public opinion against them – because they refused to answer the questions, it was thought they must have something to hide – and Bogart and the others came under suspicion of being Communists themselves. They felt that they were being used by the Communist Party, intent on martyrdom for the men on trial. The group broke up in some disarray and many, like Bogart, headed home. Stopping in Chicago, he declared that he had been 'ill advised, foolish and impetuous'. He clarified his position in a public statement: 'I'm about as much in

110

favour of Communism as J. Edgar Hoover. I despise Communism and I believe in our own American brand of democracy. Our planeload of Hollywood performers who flew to Washington came East to fight against what we considered censorship of the movies. The ten men cited for contempt by the House Un-American Activities Committee were not defended by us. We were there solely in the interests of freedom of speech, freedom of the screen and protection of the Bill of Rights. We were not there to defend Communism in Hollywood, or Communism in America. None of us in that plane was anything but an American citizen concerned with a possible threat to his democratic liberties.'

He later confided to Lillian Ross of *The New Yorker*, 'Roosevelt was a good politician. He could handle those babies in Washington, but they're too smart for guys like me. Hell, I'm no politician. That's what I meant when I said our Washington trip was a mistake.'

The Hollywood Ten were jailed for contempt (they were later joined behind bars by J. Parnell Thomas, convicted of fraud). Bogart had to contend with a lingering public suspicion about his own beliefs and sadly felt the need to have an article appear under his name in American *Photoplay* (March 1948), called 'I'm No Communist'. In it he credited Ed Sullivan with advising him that the American public was beginning to think he was a Red. In a shameful period of American history, the film industry's subjection to investigation and the subsequent blacklisting encouraged the worst excesses of Senator Joe McCarthy. In this dark era, Bogart had done his best to be one of the good guys, but even his best was not good enough. However, his sympathies never really shifted and he remained a liberal and a staunch Democrat.

Key Largo was shot early in 1948. As well as the box-office allure of Bogart's reunion with Bacall, the film also boasted such prominent and accomplished players as Edward G. Robinson, Claire Trevor and Lionel Barrymore. All the scenes with the principal characters were shot in the studio but Karl Freund's amazing cinematography expertly disguises the fact.

The dramatic situation was reminiscent of *The Petrified Forest*, as in this film too, a gangster and his entourage hold a group of innocent captives in a remote location, only the desert is replaced by the Florida Keys and Bogart no longer plays the central villain. Edward G. Robinson dominates the actions as the gangster while Bogart takes the nearest equivalent to the Leslie Howard role as one of his prisoners. Though Bogart has his moment of glory as the triumphant hero at the end (in a climax suggested in the novel *To Have and Have Not* and not used in Hawks' film version), his role overall was rather restricting. As in later films like *Beat the Devil* and *The Barefoot Contessa*, it placed him in the position of observer as much as participant. Added to that, in *Key Largo*, Lauren Bacall's performance is surpassed by Claire Trevor's Academy Award-winning portrayal of a drunken, faded gangster's moll.

Like Duke Mantee, Robinson's Johnny Rocco has all the benefit of a delayed first appearance, thirty minutes into the film. Before that, Bogart as Frank McCloud has arrived at the small hotel in Florida Keys to pay his respects to the family (Lionel Barrymore, Lauren Bacall) of a dead wartime comrade. He soon finds himself one of Robinson's prisoners. The gang leader is a vicious man without mercy, and it is only common sense on Bogart's part not to provoke him. Yet there is a feeble attempt to pump greater significance into a dated play (written in 1939), by presenting Bogart as a man too disillusioned to worry about Robinson or the threat he poses to society. When Robinson thrusts a gun into Bogart's hand and dares him to use it, Bogart refuses not because the gun may be empty but because Robinson's henchmen would shoot him and 'one Rocco more or less isn't worth dying for'. He is labelled a coward by Barrymore's and Bacall's characters while Robinson is represented as some dark force hovering over American life instead of a dangerous but pathetic dinosaur who doesn't know he's extinct. Lines like 'I had hopes once for a world where there's no place for Johnny Rocco' and 'Me die to rid the world of Johnny Rocco? No thanks!' attempt to convey deep-rooted despair, but fail to shake one's confidence in Bogart. His eyes take in Robinson's every move, and he bides his time as any sensible figure would in the circumstances.

Eventually, Bogart intervenes, consoling Claire Trevor after she has been cruelly humiliated by Robinson who savagely slaps her across the face three times. Forced to act as the pilot for Robinson's boat trip to Cuba, he has been slipped a gun by the grateful Claire Trevor. He manages to dispose of two of Robinson's henchmen, is helped when Robinson kills a third for declining to step out and get shot, and waits for the crime czar to show his face from below deck. Even in this final confrontation, Robinson has the dramatic edge. Bogart waits, silent, gun at the ready, as Robinson tries to bargain with him, lapsing into characteristic, Little-Caesar-style bravado in the midst of his entreaties. When Robinson finally appears, Bogart expertly guns him down and, in one striking image, brings back the boat (which is named, like Bogart's own vessel, the *Santana*), to celebrate his emergence as the hero. For the first and only time in their five films together, Bogart gets the better of Robinson. Yet, as on the previous occasions – *Bullets and Ballots, Kid Galahad, The Amazing Dr. Clitterhouse* and *Brother Orchid* – Robinson had the dominant part.

Even the romance between Bogart's character and Bacall's is limited by Robinson's domination over them, and it is very much his film. It is also a magnificently accomplished piece of studio film-making: the photography, sets, music and editing are all brilliant. But they cannot conceal the fatal lack of substance – it's really just another gangster film, despite the attempts to gain greater significance.

11

HIS OWN SKIPPER

Now that Bogart was entitled to make films away from
Warner Bros., he agreed to star in two films for Mark
Hellinger Productions, the independent company
launched by his close friend and drinking companion
Mark Hellinger in September 1947. During his
Hollywood career, the ex-Broadway columnist had
provided the story for *The Roaring Twenties*, been the
associate producer of *High Sierra*, and had just become
a notable independent producer with such hits as *The
Killers* and *Brute Force*. Then busy on *The Naked City*,
Hellinger had arranged a distribution deal with David
O. Selznick's Selznick Releasing Organisation for his
future pictures. He had Burt Lancaster and ace
cameraman William Daniels under contract.

When he needed more financial backing, Bogart
invested $25,000 and became his principal partner.
The company had purchased a hot property as a
vehicle for Bogart: Willard Motley's novel *Knock on Any
Door*, which had been a bestseller, and had been widely
read in magazine abridgements and as a newspaper
serial. Star and producer eyed the sensational young
discovery of the Broadway Play *A Streetcar Named
Desire*, Marlon Brando, as a possible co-star in the key
role of a juvenile delinquent. Hellinger also had the
rights to four of Hemingway's play stories, including
The Snows of Kilimanjaro, which he proposed to film

with Bogart starring under the direction of Jules Dassin.

But Hellinger suffered a thrombosis, then some weeks later, on 21 December 1947, the day before the new company's offices were to open, he died of a further heart attack at the age of forty-four. Bogart and Selznick tried to continue the company, but the assets had to be divided and the Hemingway material was sold off by the Hellinger estate (Fox bought *The Snows of Kilimanjaro* and filmed it with Gregory Peck). Bogart sought an experienced producer to help handle *Knock on Any Door* and other material that he retained, first approaching Jerry Wald who was interested but tied to Warner Bros. for a further two years.

Finally, Bogart selected Robert Lord, a former Warner producer and screenwriter. Lord had devised the story and had been associate producer for *Black Legion*, one of Bogart's favourite pictures, and was producing at MGM when Bogart approached him.

On 7 April 1948, Bogart, his business manager Morgan Maree and Lord formed Santana Pictures, named after Bogart's boat. Bogart was now in the position of other stars like James Cagney and John Garfield who had activated their own production companies, partly for creative freedom and partly to increase and retain more of their income.

To Jack Warner's annoyance, a financing and distributing deal was negotiated not with Warner Bros. but with Columbia Pictures. Bogart's name never appeared as a producer on any of the Santana productions – credit was given solely to Robert Lord – though he took the undertaking seriously, and involved himself in selecting the writers with whom he enjoyed working, at first. To establish Santana as a bona fide production company and not just a tax dodge, the company would in time make a couple of pictures without Bogart. But before getting down to work for his own outfit, Bogart reaffirmed his liberal credentials by campaigning with Lauren Bacall for Harry Truman in the presidential election.

The first Santana production was *Knock on Any Door*, an absorbing, hard-hitting study of juvenile delinquency filmed during the latter half of 1948. Bogart played a lawyer who defends a young hoodlum charged with murdering a policeman. His character, Andrew Morton, knows the slum environment from his own childhood before he hauled himself out by studying law at night school.

To direct the film, Bogart chose the young Nicholas Ray and to co-star in the key role of the delinquent, Nick Romano, he decided on the handsome and little known John Derek. The way the film was structured, Bogart ceded much of the dramatic limelight to Derek, and worked hard to make him shine, knowing that the story depended for its effectiveness on the young player making a strong and ingratiating impression.

The film's impact lies in the revelation that Romano did kill the cop, despite his pleasant appearance, earnest manner and swearing on his mother's life that he is innocent to persuade Bogart to take the case. In court, we side with Bogart, helped by the cheap tactics of the prosecuting attorney played by George Macready, an actor with a villainous image whom we automatically distrust. When Macready needles Derek into an admission of guilt (and then disarmingly apologises for the methods he has been forced to adopt to obtain the truth), the shocked Bogart can only plead for the mercy of the court, blaming Nick's character on society and declaring, 'Knock on any door and you may find a Nick Romano!' But it is to no avail and Bogart is left trying to console his client in the death cell with the promise of making more of an effort to help others like him.

On only his third film as a director, Nicholas Ray had to tread carefully with his star/producer. The scene in which the judge talks to the two attorneys in his chambers was written overnight to replace another scene in a different setting. Said Ray (interviewed in *Movie*, issue 9): '... it was the only scene about which Bogart and I had an argument. And he said "Oh, all right, if you can get the set built by tomorrow, we'll try it, otherwise we'll do it the way it's written." So I got it built in time and worked all night on the script and we shot it that way the next day.' Added Ray: '... I thought that Bogart's last speech was a particular triumph for Bogart because the master shot on it was done all in one take and when I faced Bogart with doing it all in one take, he said "I haven't said more than three lines at one time for fifteen years without a cut" and I think it was originally about a seven- or eight-minute speech. He was a wonderful actor.'

Bogart's character is more complex than might have been expected. He makes heroic gestures, like ignoring the advice of his employers that taking the case might damage his career, but he also carries a nagging guilt about not having done enough in the past and being too impatient with Nick over his difficulties. He was even given a personal life: a happy marriage and evenings spent playing chess. All in all, Bogart the actor was playing a more average man than he usually did. The film's stark outcome was to be in line with Bogart's next three productions, all of which carried downbeat endings.

Knock On Any Door was commercially and critically successful but the next Santana production, *Tokyo Joe*, merely made money. Bogart's character, called Joe Barrett, is a Rick Blaine type from the Orient, the proprietor of 'Tokyo Joe's', a Japanese nightclub, until the outbreak of war when he becomes a celebrated fighter pilot on the Allied side. Returning to occupied Japan after the war, he is relieved to find that his White Russian wife Trina (Florence Marly), is alive, but disturbed to learn that she was forced to make propaganda broadcasts by the Japanese under threat of losing their daughter and that she has a new husband (Alexander Knox). To protect her from exposure and arrest, he agrees to the demands of Baron Kimura (Sessue Hayakawa), and starts a small airline as a cover for illegal activities. The evil Baron kidnaps his daughter to ensure that he smuggles three Japanese war criminals back to their homeland. Bogart turns them over to the American authorities, rescues his child, but is shot in the process. He dies believing he will be able to pick up his life with his wife and child, but this 'tough' ending is too little and too late to redeem a plodding and clichéd narrative.

Tokyo Joe went into production early in 1949, shortly before Bogart celebrated a new production at home, the birth (on 6 January) of his first child. He was called from the set and waited twelve hours at the hospital for the delivery. The baby was named Stephen Humphrey Bogart (the Stephen came from 'Steve', the name by which Bacall had addressed Bogie in *To Have and Have Not*). Besides *Tokyo Joe*, there was another Santana picture made that year. Though called *And Baby Makes Three*, it didn't echo the Bogarts' new domestic situation and was one of the films in which Bogart didn't appear. It starred Barbara Hale as the divorcee, about to remarry, who finds she is pregnant by her former husband (Robert Young).

Bogart was beginning to discover the frustrations of being an independent producer as he made one of several unsuccessful bids for properties, only to find that the major studios had deeper pockets and could outbid him. He failed to acquire the film rights to Sidney Kingsley's play *Detective Story*, a tragedy about a fanatical policeman, which was made into a successful film by William Wyler at Paramount with Kirk Douglas in the leading role.

Chain Lightning is the most negligible of all Bogart's

later films, made under his film-a-year contract with Warner Bros. It took more than sixty days to shoot after it began production on 16 May 1949. In it Bogart plays the part of Matt Brennan, a pilot who is hired to test new jet planes being built by an unscrupulous manufacturer (Raymond Massey). At a party he is startled to see an old flame (Eleanor Parker), and a *Casablanca*-style flashback recalls their wartime romance and the misunderstanding that kept them apart. Bogart is most effective with the bitter explanatory scene: how he wrote to her twice but never posted the letters, how his postwar life had been a failure so he had nothing to offer her. Now she's the mistress of Richard Whorf's aircraft designer who dies on a test run when the ejection equipment fails to release him from the plane before it crashes. Bogart has a meaty scene listening to the tape of the inventor's last words and squeezing the glass in his hand to pieces as the moment of ground impact is heard on the recording.

Bogart gives a fine, fierce speech, refusing to make a new test of the equipment as the inventor's last words implore him to do: 'He had immortality right in his fist … but I'm alive and I'm going to stay alive.' Naturally, he does fly the test in the end and this time the equipment works. He has a flippant explanation for his use of the ejection seat – he tells Eleanor Parker in the final clinch, 'It was the quickest way to get down to you.'

When a film has dull flying sequences with a solitary pilot in the cockpit covered in headgear, it helps to have an actor with Bogart's expressive eyes glancing about and checking the apparatus. The picture is really a *China Clipper* of its time, relying on a topical situation to make up for a deficient script. Its original story was by the blacklisted Lester Cole, one of the Hollywood Ten, sheltering under the pseudonym of J. Redmond Prior.

Later in 1949, Bogart hit the headlines with a nightclub incident at New York's El Morocco that revived his rough-house reputation of the Methot years. In the early hours of 29 September, an actress called Robin Roberts tried to pick up a giant toy panda he was carrying as a gift for his son, and Bogart pushed her away. She claimed he had bruised her but was unsuccessful in a legal suit for $25,000 damages. When Bogart was asked in court if he had been drunk at the time, he replied: 'Isn't everybody at three in the morning?'

This was one of Bogart's busiest years, as he also starred in his third Santana production, the remarkable *In a Lonely Place*, with Nicholas Ray again directing. This took the violent side of the Bogart persona, detached from the usual gangster/crime milieu, and relocated it in the stress of Hollywood to investigate a murder.

Violence – the argument of the professional criminal and valid option for the hero in a tight spot – here becomes an irrational, irresistible force that can destroy an ordinary man. There are no cosy explanations (like wartime experiences or a troubled childhood) for Bogart's violent temper as screenwriter Dixon Steele. It is obvious, though, that his contempt for the hack work he has been doing is a contributing factor and the calming influence of a patient and loving woman (Gloria Grahame), who provides a climate in which he can work creatively, makes him happy and peaceful.

Because of his violent past (he broke a former girlfriend's nose in a quarrel), Bogart's character is a prime suspect when a girl is found strangled shortly after leaving his apartment. He uses his imagination to show a policeman friend (Frank Lovejoy) how the murder might have been committed and is so persuasive that he increases the suspicions of the police. Bogart's manner of love-making with Gloria

Grahame is a disturbing exaggeration of love scenes in previous Bogart movies: when he locks her head in a vice-like grip with his fingers round her neck, he could as easily be going to strangle her or break her neck as kiss her. She tries to make him take a rest from a marathon stretch of writing and he reacts by seizing her and forcing her away. His outburst is a comic one but she is momentarily taken aback and he again indicates how violence is a characteristic mode of expression for this character.

Bogart's character is under continuing pressure from the police, and only Gloria Grahame's cries prevent him from beating to death a boy motorist with whom he has nearly collided on a winding road at night. Grahame's character inevitably concludes that Bogart could be the murderer and tries to disengage herself from him.

As in other films, Bogart reacts explosively to any kind of deceit. He punches his friend and agent (Art Smith) in the face for a well-intentioned act that Bogart regards as underhand. As in the case of the motorist, he regrets his actions and tries to make amends. When he finds that Grahame has secretly arranged to run off after she has agreed to marry him, he is enraged and attempts to strangle her. Only the insistent ringing of the telephone brings him to his senses, just as her alarmed cries saved the motorist. The police find out that Bogart was not the killer and apologise for their harassment, but it is too late: Bogart walks off alone to a very uncertain future.

In a Lonely Place must have been disconcerting for the star's followers as it lacked the kind of melodramatic conclusion customary for a story with a murderer on the loose. The film was too honest, painful and off-beat to fare well commercially. Under Nicholas Ray's sensitive handling, Bogart was stretched further than he was normally accustomed to: his performance is searingly honest and the film represents one of his finest acting achievements.

However, he didn't like it very much, in part because Warners, who had Lauren Bacall under contract, had refused to loan her for the role Gloria Grahame played. The studio was still piqued that he had deserted them for Columbia. At least he was able to team up with his wife for the benefit of radio listeners in a *Screen Guild Theatre* version of *The Maltese Falcon*, broadcast on 18 May 1950.

In the summer of that year, to fulfil his contract for a film a year at Warners, Bogart agreed to make *The Enforcer*, released in Britain as *Murder Inc*. His return to film-making after a gap of eight months, it proved to be an excellent picture. (Though direction is credited to Bretaigne Windust, much of it was apparently handled by Raoul Walsh.) A cleverly constructed, gripping exposé of an organisation in the business of murder, it explained the terminology of 'hits' and 'contracts' and had Bogart as its only star name in a role that didn't really require a star. His part, as Martin Ferguson, the Assistant District Attorney heading an investigation team, is not that taxing nor substantially developed. We never know for instance if he's married or what his interests are outside of work. Showier roles went to Ted de Corsia and Zero Mostel, as terrified betrayers of the organisation, and Everett Sloane who is ultimately introduced as its evil mastermind.

Bogart's character concentrates on dogged team-work for most of the film and is only belatedly permitted to perform some solitary heroics. Then we see the old Bogart at a dockland rendezvous with the fear-stricken Ted de Corsia. Later, collecting a vital witness from a telephone box, he spots a waiting killer (Bob Steele), in the reflection of the glass door as he opens it and whirls to shoot him down as effectively as he disposed of the same actor in *The Big Sleep*. This climax takes some contriving: Bogart improbably dispatches all the police help in the wrong direction in the hope of drawing off the watching killers, then goes alone to the witness's hiding place, taking a gun offered to him by a police captain.

Following this film, Bogart took Santana into radio, making a half-hour adventure series called *Bold Venture*, which was broadcast by independent stations during the winter of 1950–51. The star portrayed Slate Shannon, owner of a run-down Havana hotel who operates a boat called *Bold Venture* for various somewhat shady enterprises. Lauren Bacall co-starred as Sailor Duvall, a woman who has been placed in his care.

At the end of 1950, Bogart undertook the last fully fledged Santana film production. This was *Sirocco*, which he claimed Columbia forced on him (Harry Cohn was anxious to get another picture out of Bogart after nearly a year). Evidently the studio saw a potential *Casablanca* in *Sirocco* but critics recognised the similarities and naturally slammed the new film as a feeble imitation. Bogart is Harry Smith, a man who earns a precarious livelihood in French-governed Damascus in 1925 by running guns to the Syrian rebels. Criticised for his lack of morals and political convictions, Bogart replies, 'I've had them – they're left behind in America with my first wife.' The French, under their intelligence chief (Lee J. Cobb), spoil Bogart's relationship with the rebels and he takes an interest in the Frenchman's mistress (Marta Toren) in revenge.

Bogart's character then makes a deal with Cobb: if he gets a pass to Cairo, the Frenchman meets the rebels' leader. Bogart is about to leave when he is asked to help rescue Cobb who is being held by the Syrians. On learning that Cobb has arranged for his girl to leave for Cairo as well, because he did not expect to return, Bogart is impressed enough to save the man. The film has a grimly ironic conclusion: Bogart is blown to bits by a hand grenade; very possibly one of those he himself slipped to the rebels. The atmosphere of bleak pessimism would have suited many French film-makers (like Clouzot), but it seemed completely synthetic when dispensed by Hollywood.

It wasn't an ending that satisfied Bogart. 'Santana has had eleven writers on *Sirocco* and none of them goons has come across with an ending yet,' Bogart is quoted as complaining to Lillian Ross in her book *Picture.* 'Too many business worries,' he added. 'With Santana, I'm bowed down with business worries.'

Bogart planned to star in another Santana picture during 1951, playing a modern adventurer in *Canela*, based on an original story by Vincent Evans (one of the writers of *Chain Lightning*). Lauren Bacall was announced as his co-star but the film was never made. He also sought to buy the film rights to Herman Wouk's new novel, *The Caine Mutiny*, but lost out to producer Stanley Kramer.

All these unfulfilled hopes and plans took up time and money, and the business worries became too much for Bogart. The year marked the end of his active producing career for Columbia, and Robert Lord left soon after the company had made one further picture without Bogart. Called *The Family Secret*, it starred John Derek as a youth responsible for the death of his best friend in a brawl, and Lee J. Cobb as Derek's attorney father who conceals his son's guilt and defends the man falsely accused of the killing.

Bogart was still under contract to Warner Bros. which restricted his availability for other work while he considered the various projects the studio put forward. They were unable to agree on suitable subjects in 1951 and 1952. In 1953, Jack Warner wanted Bogart to play opposite Judy Garland in the planned remake of *A Star Is Born.* Bogart had often run a 16mm print of the 1937 version with Janet Gaynor and Fredric March and was invariably reduced to tears by the fate of the washed-up actor, Norman Maine, married to a much younger star. It made him worry about going the same way himself. Whether he would have accepted the part proved immaterial as Judy's domineering husband, Sid Luft, insisted on recruiting James Mason instead.

With no other suitable project to hand, Bogart's contract with Warners was terminated by mutual consent in September 1953, from which date he became a completely freelance actor.

12

OSCAR AND AFTER

C. S. Forester's novel *The African Queen* had first appeared in 1935 and its film potential had long been evident. John Huston had tried to launch it with Bogart and Bette Davis at Warner Bros. in the late Forties, but Bette's abrupt departure from the studio helped to scuttle that idea. Huston himself left the studio to form an independent production company, Horizon, with Sam Spiegel (then in his S.P. Eagle phase), and they purchased the screen rights from Warners for $50,000. Bogart invested his salary in the production and was reputedly given a thirty-per cent interest in the profits.

If *The African Queen* now seems too slight for its high reputation, it still has considerable charm. Though a little too self-conscious, a little too sure of its emotional gambits, and too dependent upon the comic and sentimental aspects, nevertheless it was a bold undertaking, photographed under arduous conditions in the Belgian Congo from May to July 1951 (followed by six weeks work in London at the Isleworth Studios). Doubles, model boats and travelling mattes are evident in the finished film, but less obvious are the rubber leeches on Bogart's body: they looked so realistic that, as director John Huston jested, they may have clinched his Oscar for the year's best acting performance.

Though Marlon Brando was expected to win the Oscar for *A Streetcar Named Desire*, his disrespect for the Hollywood establishment counted against him, and

Bogart, whose anti-Hollywood barbs had never been taken too seriously, won because the part magnified (even distorted) the acting skills he had been displaying for years. He could never have picked up an Oscar for playing a private eye or gangster as that wouldn't have looked dignified. He should have been nominated at least for his depiction of paranoia in *The Treasure of the Sierra Madre*, but, like John Wayne years later with *True Grit*, he won for an uncharacteristic, expansive and showy performance as a brave *little* man. Still, he was overdue for an Oscar, and which role he won it for is not important.

His co-star Katharine Hepburn was no stranger to 'attraction of opposites' casting; probably only Huston's fondness for Bogart kept Spencer Tracy from appearing with her again. The contrast between her character – a missionary's prim sister – and Bogart's grimy, unshaven, gin-soaked, cigar-puffing skipper of a small river boat in German East Africa in 1914 is cleverly exploited. Hepburn determines to avenge her brother's death by using Bogart's boat, *The African Queen*, to torpedo a German gunboat and she bullies the hapless Bogart into agreeing to her plan. Her ruthless treatment of Bogart's character – ostracisation and gin-deprivation – is funny because it would be unbearable otherwise. Bogart's weaknesses are (according to tradition) regarded as sympathetic ones and Hepburn's pouring away of his alcohol while he has a hangover so that he can't protest effectively, is one of the most sadistic acts ever filmed. Still, the liberation of spirits continues in a happier sense when Hepburn lets her hair down and Bogart rises to the heroic demands of the occasion.

Though Bogart's Charlie Allnut is a Canadian, he was a Cockney in C.S. Forester's novel and traces of that are more than apparent in both dialogue and interpretation: Bogart's moments of deference to Hepburn seem based on class differences and his lack of breeding. The actor discards his normal, strong screen image and goes so far in the opposite direction as to appear humble and earnest. The afternoon tea scene is a case in point. Bogart sits with unusually upright posture, on best behaviour with Hepburn and Robert Morley (the missionary), but is embarrassed by his rumbling tummy. He nervously glances around and raises his eyebrows before milking the stomach gag for a final laugh, saying, 'Ain't a thing I can do about it,' with a slight shrug and a cute look which shows how little he really cares about his stomach's unruly behaviour.

Bogart was not enthralled by the location work in the Belgian Congo. As John Huston recalled in his 1980 autobiography, *An Open Book*, 'Bogie didn't care for Africa. Unlike Katie, he didn't look on this as an adventure. He never went out with me on a hunt. He preferred to sit in camp, drink in hand, and tell stories. I suspect he would never have gone to such a place as Africa with anyone else but me. With Bogie, it wasn't so much where you acted as how you acted, and he'd just as soon have been at home. He liked the London or Paris night-life scene, but when it came to acting, he saw no reason why it couldn't be done in comfort in the studio.'

Bogart thought enough of the picture and its prospects to embark on a tour of American cities in support of its openings. When he received his Oscar from Greer Garson at the Awards Ceremony, held on 20 March 1952 at the RKO Pantages in Hollywood, he said: 'It's a long way from the heart of the Belgian Congo to the stage of the Pantages Theatre and I'm glad to say I'd rather be here.'

Bogart had always enjoyed the company of journalists and so he looked with favour on the script of *Deadline USA* (released as simply *Deadline* in Great Britain). It was written by Richard Brooks, who had collaborated with Huston on *Key Largo*, had become a friend of Bogart and was now directing his own scripts. Much of the film was shot in the actual offices of the *New York Daily News*, and Bogart studied the atmosphere there before shooting began on 12 November 1951.

Faced with the sale of his paper to a rival and its subsequent demise, Bogart's Ed Hutchinson mounts an attack on a racketeer in the hope of justifying its continued existence. There is little actual action but reams of talk. One feels that Brooks was too serious to tell his story as a variation on a conventional crime-busting yarn, but not skilful enough to make his story and characters absorbing without these livelier elements.

Bogart's character's domestic difficulties – a wife who left him and is intent on remarrying – seem very trite, and too often he seems a mere mouthpiece for a free and competitive press. Bogart delivers one impassioned speech in memorable style, making a plea for the employees and readers who have rights in a paper as much as the financial owners: '*The Day* is more than a building – it's people! Fifteen hundred men and women whose skill, heart, brains and experience make a great newspaper possible. We don't own one stick of furniture in this company but we, along with two hundred and ninety thousand people who *read* this newspaper, have a vital interest in whether it lives or dies.' He supported Brooks in opposing 20th Century-Fox's attempts to remove the argument as too controversial.

Bogart continued working with Brooks, this time at MGM on *Battle Circus*, which began production on locations in Virginia on 21 July 1952. Another damagingly poor follow-up to his Oscar-winning performance, it was the only feature he made during 1952. Too much of his time was being taken up giving due consideration to the films that Warner Bros. proposed under his one-a-year contract. In 1952, these included a gambling drama, *The System*, which eventually went ahead with Frank Lovejoy in the lead.

Battle Circus dwelled on some trivial romantic complications between a M.A.S.H. surgeon, Major Jed Webbe (Humphrey Bogart), and a nurse (June Allyson) during the Korean War. The realistic backdrop of suffering in wartime jars intolerably with the slick dialogue and routine characterisations. Allyson has high ideals which are predictably shattered by her harrowing duties and Bogart clutches the bottle to forget an unhappy marriage, congratulating Allyson on becoming 'a true veteran' when she decides that wars are senseless rather than righteous endeavours.

Brooks himself later said (in *Movie* 12, Spring 1965), '... the thing that was wrong with *Battle Circus* was that always there had to be a non-motivated love story attached to a piece of material ... the point I was going to make, and in the end never made, was that the Bogie character was never really good enough to make it in the outside world. He had to make it there, where all the other problems were simplified. But the movie became a matter of whether he got June Allyson or not. Her identification with the men who were fighting and dying "somehow" became the theme. It turned out as just a plain adventure story.'

During production, Bogart was also filmed promoting Series E Savings Bonds for the U.S. Government, and his sales pitch was shown in American theatres in the last week of July.

On 23 August 1952, as shooting was coming to an end, Bogart became a father again, this time of a daughter named Leslie Howard Bogart after the star who had helped so much with *The Petrified Forest*.

Lauren Bacall became a fervent supporter of Adlai Stevenson, the Democratic candidate in the presidential election of that year; Bogie was keen on General Eisenhower, the Republican nominee, and had even gone to a fund-raising rally in Denver, but she won him over and they went campaigning for Stevenson in San Francisco, Chicago and New York, making speeches, attending lunches and joining processions. Eisenhower was by far the popular favourite in Hollywood, especially among the studio bosses, and such was the illiberal climate which still persisted there that the Bogarts were advised to shut up if they didn't want to harm their careers. Robert Ryan was one of the few others who stood up for Stevenson. After voting in California, Bogart and Bacall flew to join Adlai at the Governor's mansion in Springfield, Illinois, as the results came in and Eisenhower romped home.

Although Bogart acted in only one feature in 1952, he did record three final drama shows for American radio audiences. On 10 February, he and Lauren Bacall co-starred in *The Traitor* for NBC's *Theatre Guild on the Air*. Based on a play by Herman Wouk, author of *The Caine Mutiny*, it presented Bogart as a scientist involved with Russian spies. Then on 3 May he was heard on CBS's *Stars in the Air* in an adaptation of the Fox thriller *The House on 92nd Street* with Keefe Brasselle (over the years he had starred in radio versions of two other Fox films in which he hadn't appeared: *Moontide* with Virginia Bruce in 1945 and *13 Rue Madeleine* with William Lundigan in 1948). Finally, on 15 December, CBS's *Lux Radio Theatre* broadcast *The African Queen* in which Bogart played opposite Greer Garson. The casting changes in some of these radio adaptations gave intriguing indications of how roles would have fared in other hands.

Lacking the money himself, John Huston persuaded Bogart to reactivate his production company and purchase for $10,000 the rights to a novel, *Beat the Devil*, written by Huston's old pal, Claude Cockburn, under the pseudonym of Paul Helvick. Originally conceived as straight melodrama in an unsuccessful screnplay by Anthony Veiller and Peter Viertel, *Beat the Devil* was being hurriedly converted to satire by Truman Capote as production commenced in Italy at Ravello, a picturesque small town perched on cliffs above Amalfi.

On the night of Friday 7 February 1953 when Bogart was accompanying Huston from Rome to Ravello by car, they were badly shaken in an accident. 'Our Italian driver came to a fork in the road which had so many signs he couldn't decide to turn left or right,' Bogart later recalled. 'His solution was to go straight on until stopped by a stone wall. Huston came up laughing and I came up with two teeth knocked loose.' According to Huston, Bogart bit through his tongue and dislodged the full bridge of his front teeth. The week it took to repair the damage to Bogie gave Huston and Capote some breathing space to knock more of the script into shape.

Beat the Devil was in production for over ninety days (more than twice its original schedule), and, while the result never seems to amount to anything much, the film proves to be full of small touches and a European sophistication that make it a connoisseur's delight. At the time, however, it was a failure at the American box-office. *Beat the Devil* is perhaps best savoured as a sequel to or remake of *The Maltese Falcon* (but hardly the kind of film Warners envisaged when it seriously investigated making *The Further Adventures of the Maltese Falcon* back in 1942).

This, then, can be seen as Bogart accompanying the Fat Man and friends on another elusive quest for wealth, one that takes them from Italy to Africa. The international rogue's gallery consists of a rotund English health fanatic (Robert Morley in place of the late Sydney Greenstreet), a skinny Italian (Marco Tulli), a German from Chile with the name of O'Hara, continually mispronounced 'O'Horror' (Peter Lorre), and a fascist British major equipped with bowler hat

(Ivor Barnard, in lieu of Elisha Cook Jr.). Bogart plays their front man and an amused onlooker, Billy Dannreuther. Like Sam Spade, he handles the women: his busty Italian wife (Gina Lollobrigida) and a flirtatious blonde (Jennifer Jones), the spouse of a bogus English aristocrat (Edward Underdown), who lies with the gushing aplomb and fertile imagination of a Brigid O'Shaughnessy, but is no better at fooling Bogart than Mary Astor.

The film details the comic catastrophes that beset the motley bunch in their attempts to acquire African land rich in uranium, at a cheap price. Bogart is the only honest one amongst them, so he is naturally disbelieved when he talks of his former wealth. But he is not beyond a tall tale as is shown by his promise to an Arab administrator to arrange an introduction to Rita Hayworth in return for the band's escape from the Arab's clutches (it's a kind of half-truth as we can't help reflecting that Bogart himself could have easily ensured the introduction).

Bogart evades the handcuffs clapped on the rest of the bunch by Inspector Jack Clayton of the Yard (Bernard Lee). (The irreverent use of the name of the film's associate producer was an old gag of Bogart's: in *In a Lonely Place* the murderer was given the name of that film's associate producer, Henry S. Kesler.) The film concludes with Bogart's hearty laughter as he reads a telegram from the phoney aristocrat who has outwitted the lot of them. 'Oh, this is the end!' gasps Bogart, and it is.

In reality, Bogart was not so amused, claiming that only 'phonies' could find the film amusing and that it was a 'mess' – harsh words for such a brave departure from the norm but he had been irked by the delays caused by rewriting and by escalating costs. He had also had to go to Italy without his wife, the first time they had been separated since their marriage (she had resumed her career with a plum part in *How to Marry a*

Millionaire). Though not directly concerned with the daily administration of the picture (which was handled by British and Italian co-producers), he had been persuaded to put nearly half a million dollars of his own money into its production, and that was no joking matter. His old employer Jack Warner enjoyed his discomfort and liked to tell people that they would have difficulties keeping awake during the film without toothpicks to keep their eyes open. It is not altogether surprising that *Beat the Devil* was the Santana company's last venture although Bogart did not entirely rule out making another film with Columbia.

Post-production for *Beat the Devil* was done in London and Bogart was back in Hollywood when his voice was needed for a few additional lines, so an expert mimic by the name of Peter Sellers filled in. Bogart did provide a visual souvenir of his time in London by making an unbilled, nonspeaking appearance as himself at the end of a comedy, *The Love Lottery*, starring his good friend David Niven. And, back in Hollywood, he contributed his voice anonymously to *A Star Is Born* while visiting Judy Garland during a recording session: 'As a good-luck gesture for Judy he dubbed in the voice of a drunk in a brief sequence in a café. His voice can be heard calling for her to sing "Melancholy Baby". A stand-in was used in the actual filming but Bogart's voice remained!' So reports Al DiOrio Jr. in his 1974 Garland biography, *Little Girl Lost*.

Stories of the sea had a particular appeal to Bogart and he had coveted the role of the fisherman in Ernest Hemingway's *The Old Man and the Sea* since reading its magazine serialisation in 1952; but Spencer Tracy was even more determined and formed a production partnership which acquired it (although Tracy didn't make the film for several years). And then there was

Herman Wouk's *The Caine Mutiny*, which Bogart had sought to buy for Santana in 1951. In this case, he had the consolation of being offered the lead in the film version by producer Stanley Kramer after making plain his interest. Many other actors had eyed the role of the disturbed disciplinarian, Captain Queeg, but the film's distributor, Columbia, would have insisted on Tyrone Power if Bogart had not been willing and available.

The delays with *Beat the Devil* meant that he had to rush straight into shooting *The Caine Mutiny* in the summer of 1953. Once again, he had to travel to shoot some scenes, though a week in Hawaii consisted of only one day's filming, leaving several days for teaching his son Stephen to swim.

The director was Edward Dmytryk, who had been one of the Hollywood Ten. He had gone to prison and then given evidence to the Committee, had been 'cleared' and thereby enabled to resume his career. 'I don't give a damn what his politics were,' declared Bogart. 'He's satisfied the government that he's okay now, and that satisfies me.'

Though the drama of *The Caine Mutiny* was compromised by a romantic interest as well as comic relief, Bogart himself was razor-sharp as the captain who takes over a destroyer from a slack commanding officer and attempts to run it by the book. Worn out by past stresses, his Queeg becomes stubborn about small matters of discipline and antagonises the other officers who resist his plea for sympathy, co-operation and understanding. He is a grim but pathetic character who affirms that his wife, child and dog are 'rather fond' of him even if no one else is, but most of the incidents which cause dissension (Queeg closing down a Hopalong Cassidy film show because he wasn't notified of it and searching for keys that might have been cut to raid the ship's store for strawberries), seem to have been copied from some service comedy more suitable for Fred Clark or Paul Ford. More astringent handling by Dmytryk might have countered this impression; but these and other incidents confirm that Queeg is unfit to command and that the men are right to relieve him of his duties, after he seizes up mentally during a typhoon.

The film might have been more stimulating had Queeg been more ambiguous or cunning, or if (like the play drawn from the book) it had shown only the court-martial, leaving us to judge from the witnesses' testimony until the final scene when Queeg comes apart before our eyes. This happens while Queeg is giving evidence at the court-martial of the officer (Van Johnson) who took over the ship. Bogart shows the captain, confident and eager to co-operate, suddenly coming unstuck as he wrestles with the contradiction between the glowing fitness report he has filed on Johnson and the allegations he has made about the man being continually unreliable. When he learns that further testimony which will demolish his case is available, he reaches for the ball-bearings he carries in his pocket and starts to click them in his hand.

In a close-up of Bogart's distraught face his pent-up frustrations find expression in denouncing the other officers, then his eyes dart around to confirm his realisation that he has given himself away. This disintegration is a little too easily precipitated by Jose Ferrer as the defence lawyer, but Queeg's situation is handled with some sympathy. Both the writing and Bogart's performance make Queeg a memorable figure: vulnerable, paranoid, and pathetic.

As in *Knock on Any Door*, Bogart delivered long speeches in single takes. He also worked on his part, and in one typical instance tried to make a scene at the breakfast table more interesting by repeatedly buttering a piece of toast to show his agitation. The film's technical advisor, a naval commander, objected on the grounds that an Annapolis man like Queeg would cut up a slice of toast before buttering it, but Bogart declared his experience told him otherwise. Shooting stopped as the argument continued and Stanley Kramer had to come up with a compromise whereby Bogart trimmed the crusty edge from the toast before applying the butter.

Co-star Van Johnson has said, 'In *The Caine Mutiny* [Bogart] hardly spoke a word to me or the rest of the cast while shooting lasted. He became so much like the story's Captain Queeg that we all began to dislike him on and off the set.' Bogart was not the kind of actor to be consumed by his roles (he could snap out of a part in an instant), and this might have been a strategy to encourage better performances from his fellow players, but it is more likely to have been the truculence and bad humour he showed whilst making other pictures during this period.

In an interview with James Bawden (*Films in Review*, December 1985), Edward Dmytryk said of the film: 'I thought it very fine in the three-hour version. This was the one planned all along by producer Stanley Kramer. But Harry Cohn, who ruled Columbia, dictated no film of his could run over two hours because exhibitors were protesting they couldn't show long films enough times in a day. But reserved seat showings would have been perfect. We had to cut some of the courtroom sequences that worked so well. Also, establishing character scenes on the ship were trimmed so some of Queeg's actions lacked motivation. It still did well but would have been better the first way. They're always finding lost footage these days. I wonder if the three-hour version exists at all? Humphrey Bogart was nervous at first, fearing viewers wouldn't understand him and might laugh.' In fact, *The Caine Mutiny* was the second-biggest grossing film of the year in North America, after *White Christmas* but ahead of *The Glenn Miller Story*.

There was not that much risk in casting Bogart as

Queeg for he had already proved he could convey paranoia with much more subtlety in *The Treasure of the Sierra Madre* (it would have been more original, though probably not as rewarding, if Tyrone Power had tackled Queeg), but Bogart's performance led to another Oscar nomination for Best Actor. This time there was no denying that Marlon Brando deserved the Oscar (with his fourth successive nomination) for his portrayal of Terry Malloy in *On the Waterfront*. In any case, Bogart was deemed to have had his turn and the Hollywood old guard seemed to have lined up behind Bing Crosby for his performance in *The Country Girl* (another instance of a skilled veteran player making an impression in an uncharacteristic role).

Bogart lamented the intrusion of the love interest in *The Caine Mutiny* (a pity, then, that he didn't get to produce it), but he was initially flattered by an invitation to play a romantic part immediately after the naval drama. Writer director Billy Wilder wanted him for *Sabrina* (called *Sabrina Fair* in Great Britain); and he had top billing over co-stars Audrey Hepburn and William Holden. The script hadn't been completed but Bogart knew Wilder's track record and took a chance.

It brought him back to Broadway-style drawing-room comedy after all these years but he soon felt uncomfortable playing a deliberately dull character in a Homburg and Brook Brothers suit. His Linus Larrabee is a starchy Wall-Street tycoon who conducts the family affairs while William Holden, as his younger brother, fritters away his life as a playboy. When Holden takes a romantic interest in the daughter (Audrey Hepburn), of the family chauffeur instead of the well-connected socialite (Martha Hyer), who is favoured by the family, Bogart moves in to try and woo Hepburn away. He assumes that the romantic techniques of his younger days will return, dons an ill-fitting Yale sweater and sets out armed with a phonograph and an ancient record, 'Yes, We Have No

Bananas'. It required no crystal ball to detect that he would end up falling for Hepburn, but it was not so certain that he would find his love reciprocated.

The film was no high point in the career of either Bogart or Wilder, but it is extremely polished, well-structured and always watchable, belying the fact that production began without a completed script, Wilder writing and revising it (with Ernest Lehman), as he went along.

Bogart was unhappy with his role and the rewrites – he and Wilder, both practitioners of the sarcastic jibe, didn't hit it off at all well. On one occasion, after being presented with a new scene, Bogart asked Billy if he had any children and, told he had a girl aged two, asked 'Did she write this?' Bogart claimed to have a list of John Huston's top ten directors on which Wilder was not included; he mocked Wilder's German origins; and he refused to regain lost time by working past six o'clock. From Bogart's manner, it seemed to some on that picture that he had brought Captain Queeg with him. He was not invited to Wilder's gatherings after work because he was such 'bad company'.

Wilder wouldn't tell him that he got the girl in the end, while Bogart thought that the director ignored him on the set in favour of both Holden, with whom Wilder had often worked before, and Audrey Hepburn (making her second Hollywood film after *Roman Holiday*) about whom he could only bring himself to remark, 'Oh, she's all right – if you don't mind forty takes.' Wilder has claimed he found Bogart so professional and so quick to master new scenes that he devoted his time to other players more in need of his attention.

Early in January 1954, soon after finishing *Sabrina*, Bogart returned to Italy to star in *The Barefoot Contessa* (1954), for another noted writer/director Joseph L.

Mankiewicz; but just as *Sabrina* was second-rate Wilder, so *Contessa* fell short of a top-level Mankiewicz picture for lack of an adequate story. Hollywood has rarely proved capable of searching self-analysis and films about the film world tend to propagate the myths they are intent on exploding (*In a Lonely Place* is, of course, a powerful exception in as far as it is about film-making). Here, the dialogue had sparkle but the plot was unimpressive.

Bogart had the chance to play a Norman Maine-like character. His Harry Dawes is an alcoholic writer/director who sobers up to work for a playboy producer (Warren Stevens), and makes a big star out of a nightclub dancer, played by Ava Gardner. The film begins with her funeral and goes into a sequence of flashbacks, largely narrated by Bogart's character, a cynical wit who observes, 'The difference between European and American movie magnates is astonishing – there is absolutely none,' and rebukes Edmond O'Brien's sweaty publicist for using a cliché in conversation, 'You're being disloyal, Oscar, you're stealing dialogue from television!'

In another secondary role, Bogart remains an observer of the main drama. He is happily married and never considers himself in any role other than Gardner's friend and confidante, anxious to protect her from her wilder urges. When her impotent husband (Rossano Brazzi) shoots her and her lover, he tells Bogart, 'I have known for some time that there was someone; it may be a questionable compliment but I did not suspect you.' This was a comedown after the romantically rejuvenated image of Bogart in *Sabrina*.

Bogart found Ava Gardner harder to take than Audrey Hepburn. According to Ava's biographer, Charles Higham, 'He seemed to feel she was far too self-important and "royal", and he constantly tried to unsettle her in key scenes. It was all Mankiewicz could do to prevent a pitched battle between the stars on the

141

set.' According to the director himself, she was really 'terribly insecure'.

Bogart's coughing was another problem, and co-star Edmond O'Brien has recalled that 'many takes were printed simply for the lines Mankiewicz could get between the coughs'. Bogart had had a bad 'smoker's cough' for many years, ever since Lauren Bacall could remember, but it had been getting worse. It had become a particular embarrassment for Bogart when he had fits of coughing while watching plays in London and New York.

In *We're No Angels*, which was made in the summer of 1954, Bogart was happily reunited with director Michael Curtiz, and played a French convict escaping from Devil's Island as he had done on their last film together, *Passage to Marseille*. But here the treatment was comic with Bogart as a crook, and Peter Ustinov and Aldo Ray as murderers. The story told how the trio, breaking out on Christmas Eve, plan to rob a shop but stay to sort out the affairs of its dithering manager (Leo G. Carroll), and his family. The convicts are reluctant angels, laying on a Christmas dinner, and saying, 'We'll cut their throats – just as soon as we wash the dishes.' The arrival of the shop's skinflint owner (Basil Rathbone) and obnoxious offspring (John Baer), intent on causing trouble, stirs the convicts into action, helped by a pet viper.

The film is subtle in neither plot nor performance but Bogart, Ustinov and Ray work marvellously well together, not least in conducting a mock trial of Rathbone who arranges his own death (as per sentence), by appropriating the box containing their deadly pet. *We're No Angels* is one of the most consistently agreeable pictures of the mid-Fifties.

Joseph Hayes's *The Desperate Hours*, published in 1954, is a novel about three convicts on the run who terrorise a suburban family. Bogart bid for the screen rights but lost out to Paramount. On learning that William Wyler was going to direct the film version, he phoned the director.

'When Bogie rang, I assumed he must be interested in the part of the father,' Wyler recalled in 1974. 'So I said, "Sure, come on over and we'll talk about it, but are you certain you want to play a family man like that?" "Christ, no," he said. "Play that dull part? I want the gangster." "But the gangster's a kid," I said. "Does he have to be?" said Bogie. "I guess not," I said, and Bogie got the part.'

Spencer Tracy was keen to play opposite Bogart as the head of the threatened family but neither he nor Bogart would agree to take second place in the billing, so Tracy backed out, to be replaced by Fredric March. Production started on 18 October 1954 and extended to late January 1955. Joseph Hayes's stage adaptation of his story opened on Broadway in February 1955 with Paul Newman as the young gangster, Glen Griffin, and the release of the film was contractually delayed so that it did not appear until October.

Unfortunately, the film version of *The Desperate Hours* proves rather disappointing. Wyler's good taste sapped the gutsy vitality from a potentially good gangster film and the ageing of Griffin to suit Bogart removed the father hatred that in Hayes's novel had inflamed the relationship between the gangster and the head of the family, so Bogart's part was not as strong as it might have been. He leads the trio of convicts but he doesn't control them as Edward G. Robinson dominated his men in *Key Largo*. Furthermore, Fredric March's part is built up to make him a character of near equal dramatic weight, more so than Bogart ever was in *Key Largo*.

Among the convicts, Dewey Martin, as Bogart's younger brother, lays claim to audience sympathy as a likeable kid who went wrong; and Robert Middleton's hulking Kobish takes the initiative where violence and sadism are concerned. Bogart is unable to restrain his brother from going off or even to divest Middleton of a gun when he gets his hands on one. After Frank Sinatra in *Suddenly* and Edward G. Robinson in *Black Tuesday*, this Bogart was really a tame menace. He may down Fredric March with a blow to the head from a pistol butt, but he refrains from a second blow because it isn't necessary – thus the film avoids exploiting violence but at the same time makes it less terrifying and weakens the condemnation. Even Bogart's death scene on the lawn when he is riddled with police bullets is handled from a discreet, low angle and allows him only one parting wheeze: a far cry from his extravagant deaths back in the Thirties. The dialogue is continually trite and forgettable, and the lengthy film's only real dramatic assets are in the final tense twenty minutes as the police lay siege to the house. The box-office response was not up to expectations but, quite apart from its artistic shortcomings, it is possible audiences felt squeamish about the idea of gangsters invading ordinary suburban homes like theirs, and on screen there was a certain improbability in the plot device of keeping the mother and small son at home as hostages while the rest of the family are sent out to work to keep up appearances.

13

FINAL FILMS AND
BRAVE FAREWELL

In the spring of 1955, Bogart made his first and only picture in the new CinemaScope process. *The Left Hand of God* was a good example of how dreary films could be on the very wide screen unless vigorous direction combated the deadening effect of static talk scenes. This was a very simple and tediously developed story set in a remote province of China in 1947. True, Bogart's Jim Carmody has an intriguing introduction as a wiry figure, dressed in black trilby, clerical collar and ankle-length cassock, riding a mule up a mountain trail, incongruously clutching an automatic pistol; he is obviously a bogus priest but it is some time before he explains in flashback how he became the 'son' of an American-educated war-lord with a passion for gambling (an almond-eyed Lee J. Cobb). Bogart has taken a dead priest's garb to escape but retains it on reaching a mission, becoming worthy to wear it by living up to the faith of the villagers. Here his conversations with bespectacled Victor Sen Yung as his houseboy are a reminder of how much more interesting they were as sparring partners back in *Across the Pacific*.

A predictable complication has Gene Tierney as the widowed nurse who feels guilty for being attracted to a man of the cloth, a situation he encourages by staring into her eyes trying to remember the last time he walked out with a pretty girl; he amuses everyone with slips that are passed off as unorthodox, and really ingratiates himself by teaching the children to sing a Chinese version of 'My Old Kentucky Home'. His skill with dice saves the village from destruction but as a climax this lacks the kind of action one expects from a film which features a war-lord. Bogart seems too dour to be the inspirational character the script says he is, although he works hard to give Carmody as much depth as possible.

The film reunited him with director Edward Dmytryk who recently recalled, 'We shot all of that on the back lot. Bogart's health was one consideration. I can still hear that hacking cough. Then Gene Tierney began to come apart and that was bad, too. But I had Aggie Moorehead and E.G. Marshall to work with and nobody complained it didn't look like China.'

The Left Hand of God went into release ahead of *The Desperate Hours*. Now that Bogart had shown a renewed interest in playing criminals in the latter picture, he received an interesting offer from television to play Duke Mantee again in a live broadcast of *The Petrified Forest*. The casting of Lauren Bacall as the waitress and Henry Fonda as the wandering poet made it irresistible.

Major stars as a rule didn't appear in TV drama for fear of denting their big-screen appeal, although they would promote themselves and their current pictures on chat shows and in guest star appearances – Bogart, for example, had appeared on the Ed Sullivan show and on Jack Benny's comedy programme, and the Bogart family as a whole had opened their house to one of Edward R. Murrow's *Person to Person* shows.

Directed by Delbert Mann, the ninety-minute telecast of *The Petrified Forest* was transmitted on 30 May 1955, long before *The Desperate Hours* was released. 'The reason I did the show was pure nostalgia – it's really an easy role,' Bogart later said. 'All I had to do was just sit there in the corner and look tough.'

Reportedly, he was not too happy with the result. Besides his stage and film appearances as Mantee, he had played it once on radio opposite Tyrone Power and Joan Bennett (broadcast on 7 July 1940), so that his sole dramatic TV role did amount to some kind of rare achievement as it meant that he had played the same part in four different media.

Bogart felt tired during the making of what turned out to be his last film, *The Harder They Fall*, which began shooting on Monday 31 October 1955 in New York; but he was too professional to let it show in his performance. (The film was based on the 1947 Budd Schulberg novel which had been originally snapped up by RKO at the time of publication, first as a vehicle for Robert Mitchum, then with the idea of Joseph Cotten starring under Edward Dmytryk's direction.)

The Harder They Fall gave Bogart the meaty role of an out-of-work sportswriter Eddie Willis who succumbs to bait offered by callous boxing promoter Nick Benko (Rod Steiger) to help promote a South American ox (Mike Lane), with a 'powder puff punch and a glass jaw', through a series of fixed fights, to be a contender for world heavyweight. Thus Bogart smoothly betrays old trusts, wheedles for favours, lies to the press, and soothes his conscience with small gestures on behalf of the underprivileged fighters in Benko's circus.

Eventually, of course, Bogart's character can swallow no more and levels with the duped boxer, rushing him out of the country and out of Steiger's hands. Steiger and his men crowd into Bogart's humble apartment and Bogart announces he will expose the whole rotten business in print. Here is the narrow-eyed, finger-pointing, now-get-this-straight Bogart in all his assertive glory for the last time: 'You can't scare me and you can't buy me and you haven't got any other way. Nick, you're in trouble!'

As the frothing promoter departs, Bogart's wife (Jan

Sterling) pours him some coffee. He starts hammering the keys of his typewriter. His opening sentence ends the picture with a startling punch, one of the most forthright messages ever delivered by a motion picture, taking matters far beyond the specific corruption in the picture: 'Boxing should be outlawed in the United States if it takes an Act of Congress to do it.'

As crusading cinema, *The Harder They Fall* is exciting but far from convincing. It is rather more interesting in the way it catches the collision of two acting generations: Bogart of the old, Steiger of the new. Bogart was very much aware that Steiger was trying to blow him off the screen with his showy method acting, and complained that the mumbling made it difficult for him to hear his cues; but the old pro wasn't really worried. As time now shows even more clearly, Bogart is the winner of their big match; he is cool, crisp, concise, while Steiger is powerful but monotonous and overheated. (It is worth adding that, three years later, Steiger provided his interpretation of an old-time gangster in the title role of *Al Capone*, adopting a different style from Bogart and other actors of the Thirties.)

At the end of 1955, Bogart had returned to the ranks of the Top Ten box-office stars in American movie theatres for the year, his first appearance in this influential list since 1949. It may owe something to the fact that he was seen in no less than three new films during the year – *We're No Angels, The Left Hand of God*, and *The Desperate Hours* – as individually none of them broke any records. He was listed eighth, after James Stewart, Grace Kelly, John Wayne, William Holden, Gary Cooper, Marlon Brando and the Martin and Lewis comedy team, but before June Allyson and Clark Gable. It indicates clearly that Bogart was regarded as a strong box-office draw and that his career was flourishing.

There were a couple of promising films lined up for 1956. He and his wife were to team up for the first time

Left: Humphrey Bogart as Fred C. Dobbs, the prospector driven to madness and murder by the corrupting influence of gold in *The Treasure of the Sierra Madre* (1948).

bove: Humphrey Bogart with his fellow gold prospectors Tim Holt and Walter uston in *The Treasure of the Sierra Madre* (1948).

Above: Bogart stands up to the threats of Edward G. Robinson's gangster in *Key Largo* (1948). Barely discernible in the background are Harry Lewis, Dan Seymour and Thomas Gomez as members of the gang.

Above: In *Knock On Any Door* (1949), Bogart makes his address to the jury, watched by George Macready's smiling prosecutor, Barry Kelley's judge, and the accused played by John Derek.

Above: As the
neurotic and
violence-prone
screenwriter of
In a Lonely Place
(1950), Bogart
comes under the
calming influence
of Gloria
Grahame.

Above: An odd trio: Bogart gazes down on Robert Morley, Marco Tulli
and Peter Lorre in *Beat the Devil* (1954).

Above: An odd couple: Humphrey Bogart and Katharine Hepburn in
The African Queen (1951).

Right: Carried away on the witness stand, Bogart denounces the men who served under him in *The Caine Mutiny* (1954).

bove: Bogart had a supporting role to Ava Gardner in
he *Barefoot Contessa* (1954).

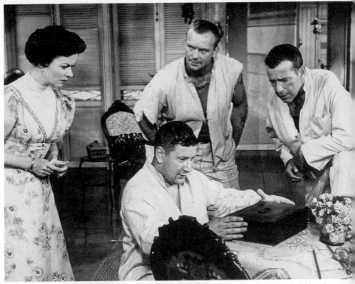

Above: In *We're No Angels* (1955), Bogart watches Peter Ustinov apply his safe-cracking skills while Aldo Ray watches a perplexed Joan Bennett.

Above: Bogart as the tough killer of *The Desperate Hours* (1955) with prisoner Fredric March comforting wife Martha Scott and son Richard Eyer.

Above: The inimitable Bogart, hero and villain to the end.

Above: In his last film, *The Harder They Fall* (1956), Bogart tells Mike Lane how he has been the dupe of boxing racketeers.

Left: Bogart sporting the characteristic fedora.

since *Key Largo* and return to Warner Bros. for *Melville Goodwin USA*, a comedy from the John P. Marquand novel. They made costume tests for a February start. After that, Bogie looked forward to some fresh air on the high seas, making a drama called *The Good Shepherd* for Columbia with Jerry Wald as producer and Ranald MacDougall (who had scripted *We're No Angels*) as writer/director. The project was derived from the new novel by C.S. Forester whose *African Queen* had served Bogart so well; this time he would play the American commander of an Allied convoy during World War II. A May start was envisaged.

Beyond that, there were various other projects that Bogart might have done, as well as an interesting one that he definitely rejected. Despite his aversion to travel, in February 1955 Bogart had signed with the Hecht–Lancaster production company, owned by Burt Lancaster and Harold Hecht, to star in a jungle adventure called *Elephantville*, to be shot in Burma or Ceylon. It was never made.

Then there was a reunion with Huston in prospect. While the script was being prepared, Huston had asked Bogart to star in *Moby Dick* but the actor was uncertain whether he could meet the challenge of playing Captain Ahab. Huston had also found new financial backing for his long cherished ambition to make a film of Rudyard Kipling's *The Man Who Would Be King* and was eager to make it after *Moby Dick*. (In due course, he did both films, the first with Gregory Peck, the second with Sean Connery and Michael Caine.)

And then Bogart had been offered, of all things, a couple of westerns. Hal Wallis wanted him for the part of the consumptive Doc Holliday in his western *Gunfight at the O.K. Corral*, but the actor had said no: a pity in some respects, because he would have been good in the part. But perhaps the role's secondary place to Wyatt Earp put him off, or the character's hacking cough and ill-health had uncomfortable parallels with his own state. (Kirk Douglas took the part and did it well.) And, secondly, Harry Cohn and Jerry Wald wanted him to play the trail boss in Columbia's film version of Frank Harris's autobiographical *Reminiscences of a Cowboy*. (That was eventually made in 1958 with Glenn Ford playing the role under Delmer Daves's direction.)

But in 1956 Bogart's health problems ruled out any prospect of work. He had been persuaded by Greer Garson to see her physician. He had been bothered by his smoker's cough for many years, but he had now lost his appetite and he consented to have a check-up. Medical examination revealed cancer of the oesophagus and immediate surgery was necessary so *Melville Goodwin USA* was postponed. On 1 March Bogart underwent a lengthy operation. Press reports referred to a 'throat obstruction'; cancer was a forbidden word. Long sessions of radiation treatment followed. Bogart was forced to withdraw from *Melville Goodwin USA* in July: the starring roles were reassigned to Kirk Douglas and Susan Hayward for a September start (the film came out as *Top Secret Affair* in 1957, and was a dud). Sam Spiegel approached him about playing in *The Bridge on the River Kwai* (in the part eventually taken by William Holden), but *The Good Shepherd* got in the way of that idea. To generate some income, Bogart sold Santana Pictures with its backlog of productions (excluding *Beat the Devil*) to Columbia for one million dollars.

Rumours that Bogart was seriously ill or dying proliferated. In October, he issued a statement to the press about 'many unchecked and baseless rumours'. He referred to 'a slight malignancy in my oesophagus' which he said had been successfully removed: 'I'm a better man now than I ever was and all I need now is some thirty pounds in weight which I'm sure some of you (the Press) could spare. Possibly we could start something like a Weight Bank for Bogart and, believe me, I'm not particular which part of your anatomies it comes from.'

It seems that Bogart did underestimate the seriousness of his condition and expected to recover or, if he wasn't going to pull through, he certainly didn't want to know. He had the Santana repainted – not the act of a man who didn't expect to use it again. He was regularly contacted by Harry Cohn, who knew he was terminally ill but generously kept up a pretence of waiting for him to make *The Good Shepherd*, postponing a September start to January 1957, and then letting the project die with Bogart.

In November, Bogart returned to hospital for a while. Allowed home, he saw old friends and kept up a bold front. He had become so weak and emaciated that he had to be shaved and dressed on a couch upstairs, then brought down in the service elevator, to a wheelchair which could carry him into the library. There he would be transferred to a chair and armed with a cigarette and a dry Martini on the rocks (whisky was too rough on his throat) to greet his guests, who included John Huston.

'No one who sat in his presence during those final weeks will ever forget,' said Huston in his eulogy at the funeral service. 'It was a unique display of sheer animal courage. After the first visit – that visit was spent getting over the initial shock – one quickened to the grandeur of it, expanded and felt strangely elated, proud to be there, proud to be his friend, the friend of such a brave man ...'

On 2 January 1957, Bogart enjoyed the Fuller/Sugar Ray Robinson championship fight on television (there was evidently no personal conviction behind the closing argument of *The Harder They Fall*). The next day, his wife declared, 'Of course he's ill, but he's not done yet ... I want his friends to know that he aims to be around for quite a while.'

But wanting was one thing, reality another. Shortly after two o'clock in the morning of Monday 14 January 1957, Humphrey DeForest Bogart died. At his own wish, there were no flowers at the memorial service on the following Thursday morning at eleven thirty at All Saints Episcopal Church on Santa Monica Boulevard in Beverly Hills where a model of the *Santana* sat prominently on display in a glass case; Bogart asked for donations to be sent to the American Cancer Society. At Warner Bros. and 20th Century-Fox, and probably elsewhere, there was a minute of silence at noon.

In his much quoted address to the mourners, John Huston also said: 'He was endowed by the greatest gift a man can have, talent... He is quite irreplaceable. There will never be another like him.' These words have stood the test of time.

A tiny gold whistle, inscribed 'If you need anything, just whistle', was interred with his ashes at Forest Lawn Memorial Park in Glendale. He had wanted the ashes spread at sea – but this wasn't permitted. He left behind him an estate worth over one million dollars and at least half a dozen of Hollywood's most memorable films.

Bogart was dead but, as John O'Hara said of the death of George Gershwin, you don't have to believe it if you don't want to. And why should you when the spirit of Bogart is still so alive, when he has become a cherished figure to so many people born since his death.

14

THE BOGIE CULT

'Miserable pain in the ass, always making trouble, always grousing that he had shit to say and everybody else had the good lines. Whined and bitched the whole shoot.' That was working with the real Bogart, according to an unidentified figure quoted by William Goldman in *Adventures in the Screen Trade*, and it confirms other reminiscences quoted earlier. It's not entirely at odds with Edward G. Robinson's remarks in *All My Yesterdays* about Bogart: 'For all his outward toughness, insolence, braggadocio, and contempt (and those were always part of the characters he played, though they were not entirely within Bogie), there came through a kind of sadness, loneliness and heartbreak (all of which *were* very much part of Bogie the man). I always felt sorry for him – sorry that he imposed upon himself the façade of the character with which he had become identified.' Robinson's point is echoed in the celebrated crack by Dave Chasen, 'The trouble with Bogart is that he thinks he's Bogart.' Yet this short, balding, grumpy figure has become a role model, a figure of legend.

As Mary Astor reflected in her autobiography, *A Life on Film*: 'Bogie had his troubles, his longing for a good world, his need to trust and believe in something. Like the rest of us. But he couldn't dismiss it with a philosophy, or stick his head in the sand. He was "aware" and he blew. Violently and often. And when he got drunk he was bitter and smilingly sarcastic and thoroughly unpleasant. The Bogart cult that has emerged is very understandable. There he is, right there on the screen, saying it loud and clear, "I hate hypocrisy. I don't believe in words or labels or much of anything else. I'm not a hero. I'm a human being. I'm not very pretty. Like me or don't like me." We who knew him well liked him. Bogie was for real.'

Of course, no person, especially a film star, behaves the same in all situations, in all moods, to all types of people, in all periods of a lifetime. Ronald Reagan, for instance, found Bogart, even pre-*Casablanca*, 'an affable, easy person, fond of gentle ribbing.'

Furthermore, the difference between the real Bogart and the image he cultivated for promotional purposes is blurred as he enjoyed playing up to the press and to some extent became what he set out to be. As a measure of his success, to politicians in an austere postwar Britain at a time when he was the screen's highest paid actor, he seemed to symbolise the frivolity of costly Hollywood imports in the argument that became popularly known as 'Bogart or bacon'.

Even after he had settled down with Lauren 'Betty' Bacall, he didn't change that much, but she helped smooth ruffled feathers. In her autobiography, Evelyn Keyes (John Huston's wife from 1946 to 1950) said of the couple, 'I liked Betty. Bogie went around acting like Humphrey Bogart, but you got used to that after a while.' The pair provided the press with colourful publicity. They were leading figures of the Beverly Hills or Holmby Hills Rat Pack (from when the Bogarts lived in the Holmby Hills district of Los Angeles), a kind of exclusive drinking and socialising circle for which Bogart was the public relations officer and devised the motto ('Never rat on a Rat'). Members included Frank Sinatra and it was the precursor of Sinatra's Clan.

Of course, the hard-boiled Humphrey Bogart of

vintage Warner Bros. pictures never went out of favour. His films were prime reissue material for movie theatres, just as they have become staples of television programming and classic videos. He was an easily accessible part of any film buff's upbringing, and one of the first stars to have his films packaged as a season or festival, as when cinemas on Britain's ABC circuit presented four of his old movies on successive Sundays (when old films were customarily shown), circa 1953.

But it was on American college campuses that the Bogart cult really took hold. In the summer of 1956, the Brattle Theatre near Harvard Yard in Cambridge, Massachusetts, routinely revived the two-year-old *Beat the Devil* and noticed that its audience of college students from Harvard, Radcliffe and MIT relished the film, in sharp contrast to the bewilderment and apathy it had earlier evoked from the bulk of American movie-goers.

The following year the Brattle Theatre booked a number of Warner Bros. films with Bogart and scored a particularly big hit with *Casablanca*. More followed before the Brattle began playing two-week Bogart Festivals. They became a fixture at mid-year exam time each winter: it became the 'cool' thing to see Bogart movies on the evening before a big exam. In January 1964, the tenth season of Bogart films – forty-seven screenings of fourteen different films – drew fifteen thousand admissions. A private club called the Club Casablanca opened on the premises; there was also a Blue Parrot Room named after Sydney Greenstreet's café in Casablanca, and a juke box that played 'As Time Goes By'.

Lines from the movies became all the rage. *Time* magazine reported: 'Harvard boys, ordering another round of drinks, rasp: "Play it again, Sam." Raising their glasses, they say: "Here's looking at ya, kid!" And when they're getting ready to blow the joint, they ask:

"Ya ready, Slim?" When they want to express arrogance or individuality, they spit: "I don't have to show you no stinking badge." That line is so popular that one group pledged to write it into examination essays, and professors were soon reading about the "stinking badge" in papers on the French Revolution.'

Bogart Festivals became the rage at revival theatres throughout the United States. *Casablanca* and *The Maltese Falcon* were the two top attractions, followed by *Beat the Devil, The Big Sleep* and *Key Largo*. Other staples were *The Treasure of the Sierra Madre, To Have and Have Not* and *High Sierra*. Audiences saw the films over and over and learned them by heart, joining in the action; when Bogie pumps lead into Edward G. Robinson at the climax to *Key Largo*, a chorus of 'More! More!' generally accompanied the sound of each shot. Films like *The African Queen* and *The Caine Mutiny*, which tampered with the tough, essential Bogart image, and which had brought him to a wider audience and showed his versatility, were not tolerated.

In Jean-Luc Godard's *A Bout de Souffle* (*Breathless*) (1960), the petty crook played by Jean-Paul Belmondo stares at a film still on a cinema frontage, pensively strokes his upper lip with his thumb, and murmurs 'Bogie' in homage to his idol: the cinema is showing Bogart's last movie, a hint of Belmondo's forthcoming demise. 'His greatest ambition is to become immortal, then die,' runs a line in the French film which is exactly what Bogart achieved.

In 1963, Bogart was the subject of the very first episode of the thirty-part *Hollywood and the Stars*. John Huston narrated the story of 'A Man Called Bogart'. The only other veteran stars given full episodes were Al Jolson, Bette Davis, Bing Crosby, and Rita Hayworth. The choices were influenced by the accessibility of film footage as United Artists, who backed the series, had control of the vintage Warner Bros. film library, but, even so, such prime time exposure helped fan the flames of Bogie worship.

A big shake-up in critical thinking, started in France, began to affect the standing of genre films, as directors like Howard Hawks gained new respect. The flood of books about the cinema helped develop this interest, and in 1965 no less than five about Bogart appeared. Suddenly Bogart was back.

And back everywhere. There is still a cinema called the 'Bogart' in Madrid, though its days of reviving his movies appear to be past. As late as 1978, and despite the number of television appearances, a double-bill of *Casablanca* and *The Maltese Falcon* was very popular at various Odeon cinemas in Britain.

One film has come to stand out from all the others: *Casablanca*. It survived being turned into a cheap 1955-56 television series under the *Warner Bros. Presents* heading, when Charles McGraw played Rick Blaine to Anita Ekberg's Ilsa Lund and Peter Van Eyck's Victor Laszlo (some of the ten episodes leaked into British cinemas as supporting featurettes). It was the first individual movie to gain the kind of cult status in the United States that later surrounded such pictures as *Harold and Maude* and *The Rocky Horror Picture Show*. In more recent years, the film has been regularly revived on the big screen in such theatres as the Drexel at Columbus and the Civic in Akron (both in Ohio), for audiences to chant the lines and many of them to turn up in costumes copied from the screen. 'Join us as we bring back an annual tradition to the Drexel,' said that theatre's May 1988 newsletter. 'Come early! You are invited to dress in "black and white", your best vintage duds or, if you're really adventurous, as a character from the movie. We'll be awarding lots of great prizes for the best dress, the most creative and the best *Casablanca* look-alikes. There'll also be contests for best impersonations of Bogart, Bergman, Peter Lorre and the rest ... if you haven't seen *Casablanca* on the big screen with a cheering audience, then we urge you to see it again (before it's colorized), and "the start of a beautiful friendship" will start all over again.'

It is, of course, the Bogart of *Casablanca* who featured in Woody Allen's hit play of 1969, *Play It Again, Sam*, advising a timid film critic on how to handle women. Jerry Lacy played Bogart, as he did in the 1972 film version of the comedy. A triangle situation like that of *Casablanca* develops, and the ending at the airport demonstrates the correct code of behaviour for Allen's characters. At the other end of the scale from this widely seen comedy, what are we to make of an obscure four-minute German short, *The Only Forgotten Take of Casablanca*? Unveiled at Cannes in 1983, it is, to judge from its synopsis, an exercise in wish-fulfilment by its maker, Charly Weller, to enlarge on the *Casablanca* myth: 'Thanksgiving Day 1942. The New York premiere of the film *Casablanca*. Humphrey DeForest Bogart noticed his favourite take [scene? shot?] was missing. It had simply been forgotten. Today, after more than forty years, the take has at last been reconstructed from the original material.'

In his autobiography, *As Time Goes By*, published in 1979, one of *Casablanca*'s writers, Howard Koch, mused over the reasons for its durability. He studied the transcripts of a series of interviews on the subject with students at Stanford University. 'I was moved by their comments because they revealed a latent idealism under the protective mask of cynicism, much like the tough-tender stance of Bogart's Rick in the film. However, the times and the political circumstances now are as different as World War II was from Vietnam. In the end Rick found an outlet for his repressed idealism, something worth a personal commitment and sacrifice. They can't, or at least haven't up to now, and our world is the worse for providing no comparable moral equivalent. One student summed up their feelings about the film in this way: "*Casablanca* shows you things you really long for. There are all those graspable values floating around in the film. It's full of a lost heritage that we can't live. Life is no longer like that." '

More recently – reflecting how *Casablanca* has become a popular icon needing no introduction – the love-making of Bogart and Bergman served as an inspiration for Kim Basinger's alien in *My Stepmother Is An Alien* (1988), while Meg Ryan's Sally of *When Harry Met Sally* (1989) put herself in Bergman's shoes to compare Bogart's merits with those of Paul Henreid as husband material. In Britain, the ghost of Bogie in *Casablanca* materialised again in the 1989 TV series *Tales of Sherwood Forest*, which featured a wine bar decorated with portrait stills from *Casablanca* and run by a Rick (played by Pete Postlethwaite), given to reveries in which he becomes Bogart in the 1942 film.

Impersonating Bogie became a profitable business for those who were good at it. Robert Sacchi challenged Jerry Lacy's earlier work in the film *The Man with Bogart's Face* (1980), based on a novel by Andrew J. Fenady. In this likeable comedy-thriller, he played a detective, Sam Marlow, who has his face remodelled by plastic surgery to make him look like Bogart, and then becomes involved in a case similar to *The Maltese Falcon*. Together with Robert Fisher, Sacchi went on to write *Bogart: A Play in Two Acts and Four Wives*, in which he again played Bogie for a twenty-month run in Los Angeles, and a 1986 reopening in Cleveland when Britt Gilder played Lauren Bacall.

A foolish rash of screen biographies included *Gable and Lombard* and *W.C. Fields and Me* (both 1976), *Bogie* (1980), and *Mae West* (1982). The latter two were unambitious television movies. *Bogie* was directed by Vincent Sherman, who had directed the real Bogart in some of his minor films, and was written by Daniel Taradash, who worked on *Knock on Any Door*. Kevin

O'Connor gave a precise but dreary portrayal of Bogart, and it could not help being a pointless exercise: if you had not seen Bogart before, this film would not inspire you to, and if you had, then you'd much rather see the real Bogart, for you cannot duplicate an original like Bogart. Then in January 1988 shooting was supposed to start on a six-million dollar feature based on a 1982 book called *Bogie and Me*, in which Bogart's hairdresser, Verita Thomson, maintained she had a secret love affair with Bogart that began in 1942 and lasted until his death.

In Britain, the Bogart look-alike industry has been dominated by Kenny Whymark. He had to be told he looked like Bogart when he was recruited to play the part in 1974 for a BBC sketch, but he subsequently improved his resemblance with a hair transplant and nose job, and is recognised by Equity as the official Bogie impersonator. For Whymark, being a bogus Bogie in television commercials for cat food, milk, paper serviettes, coffee, cassette tapes and much more, together with personal appearances opening pubs and supermarkets and the like, has become a lucrative full-time occupation.

What would Bogart think of it all? At a guess, he would have enjoyed *Play It Again, Sam*. How much, though, does the Bogart mystique owe to his early demise? The cult would not have been impossible had he survived though he might well have helped it along with some well-chosen remarks. He would not have been too old to appear in *Play It Again, Sam*. In his absence, we can thank his imitators and biographers for propagating his memory and arousing the curiosity of younger generations. But his appeal rests firmly on the films he made – they are the evidence on which future students and film enthusiasts will make up their own minds whether or not to endorse the Bogart cult.

FILMOGRAPHY

Humphrey Bogart's films are listed here in the order in which they appeared, rather than the order in which they were made. The dates are, therefore, the years in which each film was first seen and premiere dates are the earliest known showings.

The Dancing Town (1928)

Paramount Famous Lasky. Director: Edmund Laurence. Screenplay by Rupert Hughes. Two reels. Premiere: circa October. With Helen Hayes, Humphrey Bogart.

Broadway's Like That (1930)

Vitaphone – Warner Bros. Director: Murray Roth. Screenplay by Stanley Rauh. Music direction: Harold Levey. Eight minutes. Premiere: March. With Ruth Etting, Humphrey Bogart, Joan Blondell, Mary Philips.

Up the River (1930)

Fox. Director: John Ford. Staged by William Collier Jr. Screenplay by Maurine Watkins. Photographed by Joseph August. Art Director: Duncan Cramer. Editor: Frank E. Hull. Ninety-two minutes. New York premiere: October. With Spencer Tracy (St. Louis),

Warren Hymer (Dannemora Dan), Humphrey Bogart (Steve), Claire Luce (Judy), Joan Lawes (Jean), Sharon Lynn (Edith LaVerne), George MacFarlane (Jessup), Gaylord Pendleton (Morris), William Collier Sr. (Pop), Morgan Wallace (Frosby), Robert E. O'Connor (Guard), Louise MacIntosh (Mrs. Massey), Edythe Chapman (Mrs. Jordan), Johnny Walker (Happy), Noel Francis (Sophie), Mildred Vincent (Annie), Wilbur Mack (Whitelay), Joe Brown (Deputy Warden).

A Devil with Women (1930)

Fox. Director: Irving Cummings. Associate producer: George Middleton. Screenplay by Dudley Nichols and Henry M. Johnson, based on the magazine story *Dust and Sun* by Clements Ripley. Photographed by Arthur Todd and Al Brick. Art director: William Darling. Editor: Jack Murray. Seventy-six minutes. New York premiere: October. With Victor McLaglen (Jerry Maxton), Mona Maris (Rosita Fernandez), Humphrey Bogart (Tom Standish), Michael Vavitch (Morloff), Luana Alcaniz (Dolores), Solidad Jiminez (Duenna), John St. Polis (Don Diego), Mona Rico (Alicia), Robert Edeson (General Garcia), Joe De La Cruz (Juan).

Body and Soul (1931)

Fox. Director: Alfred Santell. Screenplay by Jules Furthman, based on the play *Squadrons* by A.E. Thomas from the story *Big Eyes and Little Mouth* by Elliott White Springs. Photographed by Glen Mac-Williams. Art director: Anton Grot. Editor: Paul Weatherwax. Seventy minutes. New York premiere: March. With Charles Farrell (Mal Andrews), Elissa Landi (Carla), Humphrey Bogart (Jim Watson), Myrna Loy (Alice Lester), Donald Dillaway (Tap Johnson), Crauford Kent (Major Burke), Pat Somerset (Major

Knowls), Ian MacLaren (General Trafford-Jones), Dennis D'Auburn (Lt. Meggs), Douglas Dray (Zane), Harold Kinney (Young), Bruce Warren (Sam Douglas).

Bad Sister (1931)

Universal. Director: Hobart Henley. Producer: Carl Laemmle Jr. Screenplay by Raymond L. Schrock, Tom Reed and Edwin H. Knopf, based on the story *The Flirt* by Booth Tarkington. Photographed by Karl Freund. Editor: Ted Kent. Sixty-eight minutes. New York premiere: March. With Conrad Nagel (Dr. Dick Lindley), Sidney Fox (Marianne Madison), Bette Davis (Laura Madison), ZaSu Pitts (Minnie), Slim Summerville (Sam), Charles Winninger (Mr. Madison), Emma Dunn (Mrs. Madison), Humphrey Bogart (Valentine Corliss), Bert Roach (Wade Trumbull), David Durand (Hedrick Madison).

Women of All Nations (1931)

Though Bogart is listed in the cast of this film, he was cut out prior to release.

A Holy Terror (1931)

Fox. Director: Irving Cummings. Associate producer: Edmund Grainger. Screenplay by Ralph Block, Alfred A. Cohn and Myron Fagan, based on the novel *Trailin'* by Max Brand. Photographed by George Schneiderman. Editor: Ralph Dixon. Fifty-three minutes. New York premiere: July. With George O'Brien (Tony Bard), Sally Eilers (Jerry Foster), Rita LaRoy (Kitty Carroll), Humphrey Bogart (Steve Nash), James Kirkwood (William Drew), Stanley Fields (Butch Morgan), Robert Warwick (Thomas Woodbury), Richard Tucker (Tom Hedges), Earl Pingree (Jim Lawler).

Love Affair (1932)

Columbia (through United Artists in Great Britain).
Director: Thornton Freeland. Screenplay by Jo
Swerling and Dorothy Howell, based on the magazine
story by Ursula Parrott. Photographed by Ted
Tetzlaff. Editor: Jack Dennis. Sixty-nine minutes.
Release: March. With Dorothy Mackaill (Carol Owen),
Humphrey Bogart (Jim Leonard), Jack Kennedy
(Gilligan), Barbara Leonard (Felice), Astrid Allwyn
(Linda Lee), Bradley Page (Georgie), Halliwell Hobbes
(Kibbee), Hale Hamilton (Mr. Hardy), Harold Minjir
(Antone).

Big City Blues (1932)

Warner Bros. Director: Mervyn LeRoy. Screenplay by
Ward Morehouse and Lillie Hayward, based on the
former's unproduced play *New York Town*. Photo-
graphed by James Van Trees. Art director: Anton
Grot. Editor: Ray Curtiss. Sixty-five minutes. Los
Angeles premiere: 18 August. With Joan Blondell
(Vida), Eric Linden (Buddy Reeves), Inez Courtney
(Faun), Walter Catlett (Gibbony), Evalyn Knapp
(Jo-Jo), Guy Kibbee (Hummel), Lyle Talbot (Sully),
Gloria Shear (Agnes), Jobyna Howland (Serena),
Humphrey Bogart (Shep Adkins), Josephine Dunn
(Jackie).

Three on a Match (1932)

First National (Warner Bros.). Director: Mervyn
LeRoy. Screenplay by Lucien Hubbard, Kubec
Glasmon and John Bright. Photographed by Sol Polito.
Art director: Robert M. Haas. Editor: Ray Curtiss.
Sixty-four minutes. New York premiere: October.
With Joan Blondell (Mary Bernard), Warren William
(Henry Kirkwood), Ann Dvorak (Vivian Revere), Bette
Davis (Ruth Westcott), Grant Mitchell (Gilmour), Lyle

Talbot (Mike Loftus), Buster Phelps (Junior Kirkwood), Humphrey Bogart (Harve), Allen Jenkins and Jack LaRue (Harve's henchmen), Edward Arnold (Ace), Frankie Darro (Bobbie).

Midnight (1934) (Reissue title: Call It Murder)

All-Star – Universal. Director, producer and screenplay: Chester Erskine, based on the play by Claire and Paul Sifton. Photographed by William Steiner and George Webber. Art director: Sam Corso. Editor: Leo Zochling. Seventy-six minutes (sixty-seven minutes in Britain). New York premiere: March. With Sidney Fox (Stella Weldon), O.P. Heggie (Edward Weldon), Henry Hull (Nolan), Margaret Wycherly (Mrs. Weldon), Lynne Overman (Joe Biggers), Katherine Wilson (Ada Biggers), Richard Whorf (Arthur Weldon), Humphrey Bogart (Garboni), Granville Bates (Henry McGrath), Cora Witherspoon (Elizabeth McGrath), Moffatt Johnson (District Attorney), Henry O'Neill (Edgar V. Ingersoll), Helen Flint (Ethel Saxton).

The Petrified Forest (1936)

Warner Bros. Director: Archie Mayo. Associate producer: Henry Blanke. Screenplay by Charles Kenyon and Delmer Daves, based on the play by Robert Emmet Sherwood. Photographed by Sol Polito. Art director: John Hughes. Editor: Owen Marks. Eighty-three minutes. New York premiere: 6 February. With Leslie Howard (Alan Squier), Bette Davis (Gabrielle Maple), Genevieve Tobin (Edith Chisholm), Dick Foran (Boze Hertzlinger), Humphrey Bogart (Duke Mantee), Joseph Sawyer (Jackie), Porter Hall (Jason Maple), Charley Grapewin (Gramp Maple), Paul Harvey (Chisholm), Adrian Morris (Ruby), Slim Johnson (Pyler), John Alexander (Joseph).

Bullets or Ballots (1936)

First National (Warner Bros.). Director: William Keighley. Associate producer: Louis F. Edelman. Screenplay by Seton I. Miller, based on his story written with Martin Mooney. Photographed by Hal Mohr. Art director: Carl Jules Weyl. Editor: Jack Killifer. Eighty-one minutes. New York premiere: 26 May. With Edward G. Robinson (Johnny Blake), Joan Blondell (Lee Morgan), Barton MacLane (Al Kruger), Humphrey Bogart (Nick "Bugs" Fenner), Frank McHugh (Herman), Joseph King (Capt. Dan McLaren), Richard Purcell (Driscoll), George E. Stone (Wires Cagles), Joseph Crehan (Grand Jury Spokesman), Henry O'Neill (Ward Bryant), Henry Kolker (Hollister), Gilbert Emery (Thorndyke), Herbert Rawlinson (Caldwell), Louise Beavers (Nellie), Norman Willis (Louis Vinci).

Two Against the World (1936) (in Great Britain: **The Case of Mrs. Pembrook**) (American TV title: **One Fatal Hour**)

First National (Warner Bros.). Director: William McGann. Supervised by Bryan Foy. Screenplay by Michel Jacoby, based on a story idea [play *Five Star Final*] by Louis Weitzenkorn. Photographed by Sid Hickox. Art director: Esdras Hartley. Editor: Frank Magee. Sixty-five minutes. Release: July. With Humphrey Bogart (Sherry Scott), Beverly Roberts (Alma Ross), Helen McKellar (Martha Carstairs), Henry O'Neill (Jim Carstairs), Linda Perry (Edith Carstairs), Carlyle Moore Jr. (Billy Sims), Florence Fair (Mrs. Marion Sims), Robert Middlemass (Bertram C. Reynolds), Clay Clement (Mr. Banning).

China Clipper (1936)

First National (Warner Bros.). Director: Ray Enright.

Associate producer: Louis F. Edelman. Screenplay by Frank Wead (uncredited additional dialogue by Norman Reilly Raine). Photographed by Arthur Edeson. Art director: Max Parker. Editor: Owen Marks. Eighty-five minutes. New York premiere: August. With Pat O'Brien (Dave Logan), Beverly Roberts (Jean Logan), Ross Alexander (Tom Collins), Humphrey Bogart (Hap Stuart), Marie Wilson (Sunny Avery), Henry B. Walthall (Dad Brunn), Joseph Crehan (Jim Horn), Joseph King (Mr. Pierson), Addison Richards (B.C. Hill), Ruth Robinson (Mother Brunn), Kenneth Harlan (Commerce Inspector).

Isle of Fury (1936)

Warner Bros. Director: Frank McDonald. Supervised by Bryan Foy. Screenplay by Robert Andrews and William Jacobs, based on the novel *The Narrow Corner* by W. Somerset Maugham. Photographed by Frank Good. Art director: Esdras Hartley. Editor: Warren Low. Sixty minutes. Release: October. With Humphrey Bogart (Val Stevens), Margaret Lindsay (Lucille Gordon), Donald Woods (Eric Blake), Paul Graetz (Capt. Deever), Gordon Hart (Andersen), E.E. Clive (Dr. Hardy), George Regas (Otar), Sidney Bracy (Sam), Tetsu Komai (Kim Lee), Miki Morita (Oh Kay), Houseley Stevenson Sr. (Rector), Frank Lackteen (Old Native).

Black Legion (1937)

Warner Bros. Director: Archie Mayo. Associate producer: Robert Lord. Screenplay by Abem Finkel and William Wister Haines, based on a story by Robert Lord. Photographed by George Barnes. Art director: Robert Haas. Editor: Owen Marks. Eighty-three minutes. New York premiere: 16 January. With Humphrey Bogart (Frank Taylor), Dick Foran (Ed

Jackson), Erin O'Brien-Moore (Ruth Taylor), Ann Sheridan (Betty Grogan), Robert Barrat (Brown), Helen Flint (Pearl Danvers), Joseph Sawyer (Cliff Moore), Addison Richards (Prosecutor), Eddie Acuff (Metcalf), Clifford Soubier (Mike Grogan), Paul Harvey (Billings), Samuel Hinds (Judge), John Litel (Tommy Smith), Charles Halton (Dan Osgood), Francis Sayles (Charlie), Harry Hayden (Jonesy), Alonzo Price (Alf Hargrave), Dickie Jones (Buddy Taylor), Dorothy Vaughan (Mrs. Grogan), Henry Brandon (Joe Dombrowski), Pat C. Flick (Nick Strumpas), Paul Stanton (Barham), Egon Brecher (Dombrowski Sr.).

The Great O'Malley (1937)

Warner Bros. Director: William Dieterle. Associate producer: Harry Joe Brown. Screenplay by Milton Krims and Tom Reed, based on the story *The Making of O'Malley* by Gerald Beaumont. Photographed by Ernest Haller. Art director: Hugh Reticker. Editor: Warren Low. Seventy-one minutes. New York premiere: March. With Pat O'Brien (James Aloysius O'Malley), Humphrey Bogart (John Phillips), Sybil Jason (Barbara Phillips), Frieda Inescort (Mrs. Phillips), Henry O'Neill (Attorney for the Defense), Hobart Cavanaugh (Pinky Holden), Mary Gordon (Mrs. O'Malley), Frank Sheridan (Father Patrick), Delmar Watson (Tubby), Ann Sheridan (Judy Nolan), Donald Crisp (Capt. Cromwell), Craig Reynolds (Motorist), Gordon Hart (Doctor), Frank Reicher (Dr. Larson).

Marked Woman (1937)

First National (Warner Bros.). Director: Lloyd Bacon. Associate producer: Louis F. Edelman. Screenplay by Robert Rossen and Abem Finkel (uncredited additional dialogue by Seton I. Miller). Photographed by George Barnes. Art director: Max Parker. Editor: Jack Killifer. Ninety-six minutes. New York premiere: 10 April. With Bette Davis (Mary Dwight), Humphrey Bogart (David Graham), Isabel Jewell (Emmy Lou), Eduardo Ciannelli (Johnny Vanning), Rosalind Marquis (Florrie), Lola Lane (Gabby), Jane Bryan (Betty), Mayo Methot (Estelle), John Litel (Gordon), Ben Welden (Charlie), Damian O'Flynn (Ralph Krawford), Henry O'Neill (Sheldon), Allen Jenkins (Louie), William B. Davidson (Crandall).

Kid Galahad (1937) (American TV title: **The Battling Bellhop**)

Warner Bros. Director: Michael Curtiz. Associate producer: Samuel Bischoff. Screenplay by Seton I. Miller, based on the magazine story by Francis Wallace. Music: Heinz Roemheld and Max Steiner. Photographed by Gaetano Gaudio. Art director: Carl Jules Weyl. Editor: George Amy. 101 minutes. New York premiere: 26 May. With Edward G. Robinson (Nick Donati), Bette Davis (Fluff – Louise Phillips), Humphrey Bogart (Turkey Morgan), Wayne Morris (Ward Guisenberry – Kid Galahad), Jane Bryan (Marie), Harry Carey Sr. (Silver Jackson), William Haade (Chuck McGraw), Soledad Jiminez (Mrs. Donati), Joe Cunningham (Joe Taylor), Ben Welden (Buzz Barrett), Joseph Crehan (Brady), Veda Ann Borg (Redhead), Frank Faylen (Barney), Harland Tucker (Gunman), George Humbert (Barber).

San Quentin (1937)

First National (Warner Bros.). Director: Lloyd Bacon. Associate producer: Samuel Bischoff. Screenplay by Peter Milne and Humphrey Cobb (uncredited contributions by Charles Belden, Seton I. Miller and Tom Reed, and additional dialogue by Laird Doyle), based on a story by Robert Tasker and John Bright. Photographed by Sid Hickox. Art director: Esdras Hartley. Editor: William Holmes. Seventy minutes. New York premiere: August. With Pat O'Brien (Capt. Steve Jameson), Humphrey Bogart (Joe 'Red' Kennedy), Ann Sheridan (May), Barton MacLane (Lt. Druggin), Joseph Sawyer (Carl G. 'Sailor Boy' Hansen), Veda Ann Borg (Helen), James Robbins (Mickey Callahan), Joseph King (Warden Taylor), Gordon Oliver (Captain), Garry Owen (Dopey), Marc Lawrence (Venetti), Emmett Vogan (Lieutenant), Max Wagner (Prison Runner), Ernie Adams (Fink).

Dead End (1937)

Goldwyn – United Artists. Director: William Wyler. Producer: Samuel Goldwyn. Associate producer: Merritt Hulburd. Screenplay by Lillian Hellman, based on the play by Sidney Kingsley. Music direction: Alfred Newman. Photographed by Gregg Toland. Art director: Richard Day. Editor: Daniel Mandell. Ninety-three minutes. New York premiere: August. With Sylvia Sidney (Drina), Joel McCrea (Dave), Humphrey Bogart ('Baby Face' Martin), Wendy Barrie (Kate), Claire Trevor (Francey), Allen Jenkins (Hunk), Marjorie Main (Mrs. Martin), Billy Halop (Tommy), Huntz Hall (Dippy), Bobby Jordan (Angel), Leo Gorcey (Spit), Gabriel Dell (T.B.), Bernard Punsley (Milty), Charles Peck (Philip), Minor Watson (Mr. Griswold), James Burke (Mulligan), Ward Bond (Doorman), Elizabeth Risdon (Mrs. Connell), Esther Dale (Mrs. Fenner), Marcelle Corday (Governess).

Stand-In (1937)

Walter Wanger – United Artists. Director: Tay Garnett. Producer: Walter Wanger. Screenplay by Gene Towne and Graham Baker, based on the magazine story by Clarence Budington Kelland. Music direction: Heinz Roemheld. Photographed by Charles Clarke. Art director: Alexander Toluboff. Editors: Otho Lovering, Dorothy Spencer. Ninety minutes. New York premiere: November. With Leslie Howard (Atterbury Dodd), Joan Blondell (Lester Plum), Humphrey Bogart (Douglas Quintain), Alan Mowbray (Koslofski), Marla Shelton (Cherie), C. Henry Gordon (Ivor Nassau), Jack Carson (Potts), H.C. Nugent (Pettypacker Jr.), William V. Mong (Pettypacker), Tully Marshall (Pettypacker Sr.), Esther Howard (Mrs. Mack).

Swing Your Lady (1937)

Warner Bros. Director: Ray Enright. Associate producer: Samuel Bischoff. Screenplay by Joseph Schrank and Maurice Leo, based on the play by Kenyon Nicholson and Charles Robinson. Music: Adolph Deutsch. Photographed by Arthur Edeson. Art director: Esdras Hartley. Editor: Jack Killifer. Seventy-two minutes. Los Angeles premiere: December. With Humphrey Bogart (Ed Hatch), Frank McHugh (Popeye), Louise Fazenda (Sadie), Nat Pendleton (Joe), Penny Singleton (Cookie), Allen Jenkins (Shiner), Leon Weaver (Waldo), Frank Weaver (Ollie Davis), Elvira Weaver (Mrs. Davis), Ronald Reagan (Jack Miller), Daniel Boone Savage (Noah), Hugh O'Connell (Smith), Tommy Bupp (Rufe), Sonny Bupp (Len).

Crime School (1938)

First National (Warner Bros.). Director: Lewis Seiler. Associate producer: Bryan Foy. Screenplay by Crane Wilbur and Vincent Sherman, based on a story by Crane Wilbur. Music: Max Steiner. Photographed by Arthur Todd. Art director: Charles Novi. Editor:

Terry Morse. Eighty-six minutes. New York premiere: 10 May. With Humphrey Bogart (Mark Braden), Gale Page (Sue Warren), Billy Halop (Frankie Warren), Bobby Jordan (Squirt), Huntz Hall (Goofy), Leo Gorcey (Spike), Bernard Punsley (Fats), Gabriel Dell (Bugs), George Offerman Jr. (Red), Weldon Heyburn (Cooper), Cy Kendall (Morgan), Charles Trowbridge (Judge Clinton), Milburn Stone (Joe Delaney), Harry Cording (Guard), Spencer Charters (Old Doctor), Donald Briggs (New Doctor), Frank Jaquet (Commissioner).

Men Are Such Fools (1938)

Warner Bros. Director: Busby Berkeley. Associate producer: David Lewis. Screenplay by Norman Reilly Raine and Horace Jackson, based on the magazine story by Faith Baldwin. Music: Heinz Roemheld. Photographed by Sid Hickox. Art director: Max Parker. Editor: Jack Killifer. Sixty-nine minutes. New York premiere: June. With Wayne Morris (Jimmy Hall), Priscilla Lane (Linda Lawrence), Humphrey Bogart (Harry Galleon), Hugh Herbert (Harvey Bates), Johnnie Davis (Tad), Penny Singleton (Nancy), Mona Barrie (Beatrice Harris), Marcia Ralston (Wanda Townsend), Gene Lockhart (Bill Dalton), Kathleen Lockhart (Mrs. Dalton).

The Amazing Dr. Clitterhouse (1938)

First National (Warner Bros.). Director: Anatole Litvak. Associate producer: Robert Lord. Screenplay by John Wexley and John Huston, based on the play by Barré Lyndon. Music: Max Steiner. Photographed by Tony Gaudio. Art director: Carl Jules Weyl. Editor: Warren Low. Eighty-seven minutes. New York premiere: 20 July. With Edward G. Robinson (Dr. Clitterhouse), Claire Trevor (Jo Keller), Humphrey

Bogart (Rocks Valentine), Allen Jenkins (Okay), Donald Crisp (Inspector Lewis Lane), Gale Page (Nurse Randolph), Henry O'Neill (Judge) John Litel (Prosecutor), Thurston Hall (Grant), Maxie Rosenbloom (Butch), Bert Hanlon (Pal), Ward Bond (Tug), Curt Bois (Rabbit), Vladimir Sokoloff (Popus), Billy Wayne (Candy), Robert Homans (Lt. Ethelbert Johnson), Irving Bacon (Jury Foreman).

Racket Busters (1938)

Cosmopolitan – Warner Bros. Director: Lloyd Bacon. Associate producer: Samuel Bischoff. Screenplay by Robert Rossen and Leonardo Bercovici. Music: Adolph Deutsch. Photographed by Arthur Edeson. Art director: Esdras Hartley. Editor: James Gibbon. Seventy-one minutes. New York premiere: 10 August. With Humphrey Bogart (Martin), George Brent (Denny Jordan), Gloria Dickson (Nora Jordan), Allen Jenkins (Skeets Wilson), Walter Abel (Allison), Henry O'Neill (Governor), Penny Singleton (Gladys), Anthony Averill (Crane), Oscar O'Shea (Pop), Elliott Sullivan (Charlie Smith), Fay Helm (Mrs. Smith), Joe Downing (Joe), Norman Willis (Gus), Don Rowan (Kimball), Charles Trowbridge (Judge), Robert McWade (Mouthpiece).

Angels with Dirty Faces (1938)

First National – Warner Bros. Director: Michael Curtiz. Associate producer: Sam Bischoff. Screenplay by John Wexley and Warren Duff, based on a story by Rowland Brown. Music: Max Steiner. Photographed by Sol Polito. Art director: Robert Haas. Editor: Owen Marks. Ninety-seven minutes. Los Angeles premiere: 24 November. With James Cagney (Rocky Sullivan), Pat O'Brien (Jerry Connolly), Humphrey Bogart (James Frazier), Ann Sheridan (Laury Martin), George

Bancroft (Mac Keefer), Billy Halop (Soapy), Bobby Jordan (Swing), Leo Gorcey (Bim), Gabriel Dell (Pasty), Huntz Hall (Crab), Bernard Punsley (Hunky), Joe Downing (Steve), Edward Pawley (Edwards), Adrian Morris (Blackie), St. Brendan's Church Choir.

King of the Underworld (1939)

Warner Bros. Director: Lewis Seiler. Associate producer: Bryan Foy. Screenplay by George Bricker and Vincent Sherman, based on the story *Dr. Socrates* by W.R. Burnett. Music: H. Roemheld. Photographed by Sid Hickox. Art director: Charles Novi. Editor: Frank Dewar. Sixty-nine minutes. New York premiere: January. With Humphrey Bogart (Joe Gurney), Kay Francis (Carol Nelson), James Stephenson (Bill Forrest), John Eldredge (Niles Nelson), Jessie Busley (Aunt Margaret), Arthur Aylesworth (Dr. Sanders), Raymond Brown (Sheriff), Harland Tucker (Mr. Ames), Ralph Remley (Mr. Robert), Charley Foy (Eddie).

The Oklahoma Kid (1939)

Warner Bros. Director: Lloyd Bacon. Associate producer: Samuel Bischoff. Screenplay by Warren Duff, Robert Buckner and Edward E. Paramore, based on a story by Edward E. Paramore and Wally Klein. Music: Max Steiner. Photographed by James Wong Howe. Art director: Esdras Hartley. Editor: Owen Marks. Eighty minutes. New York premiere: 10 March. With James Cagney (Jim Kincaid), Humphrey Bogart (Whip McCord), Rosemary Lane (Jane Hardwick), Donald Crisp (Judge Hardwick), Harvey Stephens (Ned Kincaid), Hugh Sothern (John Kincaid), Charles Middleton (Alec Martin), Edward Pawley (Ace Doolin), Ward Bond (Wes Handley), Lew Harvey (Ed Curley), Trevor Bardette (Indian Joe

Pasco), John Miljan (Ringo), Arthur Aylesworth (Judge Morgan), Irving Bacon (Hotel clerk), Joe Devlin (Keely), Wade Boteler (Sheriff).

You Can't Get Away with Murder (1939)

First National – Warner Bros. Director: Lewis Seiler. Associate producer: Samuel Bischoff. Screenplay by Robert Buckner, Don Ryan and Kenneth Gamet, based on the play *Chalked Out* by Warden Lewis E. Lawes and Jonathan Finn. Music: H. Roemheld. Photographed by Sol Polito. Art director: Hugh Reticker. Editor: James Gibbon. Seventy-eight minutes. New York premiere: 24 March. With Humphrey Bogart (Frank Wilson), Gale Page (Madge Stone), Billy Halop (Johnnie Stone), John Litel (Attorney Carey), Henry Travers (Pop), Harvey Stephens (Fred Burke), Harold Huber (Scappa), Joe Sawyer (Red), Joe Downing (Smitty), George E. Stone (The Toad), Joseph King (Principal Keeper), Joseph Crehan (Warden), John Ridgely (Gas Station Attendant), Herbert Rawlinson (District Attorney).

Dark Victory (1939)

First National – Warner Bros. Director: Edmund Goulding. Associate producer: David Lewis. Screenplay by Casey Robinson, based on the play by George Emerson Brewer Jr. and Bertram Bloch. Music: Max Steiner. Photographed by Ernie Haller. Art director: Robert Haas. Editor: William Holmes. 106 minutes. New York premiere: 20 April. With Bette Davis (Judith Traherne), George Brent (Dr. Frederick Steele), Humphrey Bogart (Michael O'Leary), Geraldine Fitzgerald (Ann King), Ronald Reagan (Alec Hamm), Henry Travers (Dr. Parsons), Cora Witherspoon (Carrie Spottswood), Dorothy Peterson (Miss Wainwright), Virginia Brissac (Martha), Charles Richman

(Col. Mantle), Herbert Rawlinson (Dr. Carter),
Leonard Mudie (Dr. Driscoll), Fay Helm (Miss Dodd),
Lottie Williams (Lucy).

The Roaring Twenties (1939)

Warner Bros. Director: Raoul Walsh. Executive
producer: Hal B. Wallis. Associate producer: Samuel
Bischoff. Screenplay by Jerry Wald, Richard Macaulay
and Robert Rossen (uncredited additional material by
John Wexley, Earl Baldwin and Frank Donoghue),
based on a story by Mark Hellinger. Music: Heinz
Roemheld and Ray Heindorf. Photographed by Ernest
Haller. Art director: Max Parker. Editor: Jack Killifer.
106 minutes. Mass premiere: 28 October. With James
Cagney (Eddie Bartlett), Priscilla Lane (Jean Sher-
man), Humphrey Bogart (George Hally), Gladys
George ('Panama' Smith), Jeffrey Lynn (Lloyd Hart),
Frank McHugh (Danny Green), Paul Kelly (Nick
Brown), Elizabeth Risdon (Mrs. Sherman), Vera Lewis
(Mrs. Gray), Edward Keane (Henderson), Joe Sawyer
(Sgt. Jones), Joseph Crehan (Fletcher), George Meeker
(Masters), John Hamilton (Judge), Robert Elliott and
Eddie Chandler (Detectives), Abner Biberman (Lefty),
John Deering (Narrator).

The Return of Doctor X (1939)

First National — Warner Bros. Director: Vincent
Sherman. Associate producer: Bryan Foy. Screenplay
by Lee Katz, based on the story *The Doctor's Secret* by
William J. Makin. Photographed by Sid Hickox. Art
director: Esdras Hartley. Editor: Thomas Pratt.
Sixty-two minutes. New York premiere: November.
With Humphrey Bogart (Marshall Quesne), Rosemary
Lane (Joan Vance), Wayne Morris (Walter Garrett),
Dennis Morgan (Michael Rhodes), John Litel (Dr.
Francis Flegg), Lya Lys (Angela Merrova), Huntz Hall

(Pinky), Charles Wilson (Detective Ray Kincaid), Vera Lewis (Miss Sweetman), Olin Howland (Undertaker), John Ridgely (Stanley Rodgers), Joseph Crehan (Editor), Ian Wolfe (Cemetery keeper).

Invisible Stripes (1939)

Warner Bros. – First National. Director: Lloyd Bacon. Executive producer: Hal B. Wallis. Associate producer: Louis F. Edelman. Screenplay by Warren Duff, based on a story by Jonathan Finn from a novel by Warden Lewis E. Lawes. Music director: Heinz Roemheld. Photographed by Ernie Haller. Art director: Max Parker. Editor: James Gibbon. Eighty-two minutes. Los Angeles premiere: 28 December. With George Raft (Cliff Taylor), Jane Bryan (Peggy), William Holden (Tim Taylor), Humphrey Bogart (Chuck Martin), Flora Robson (Mrs. Taylor), Paul Kelly (Ed Kruger), Lee Patrick (Molly Daniels), Henry O'Neill (Parole Officer Masters), Frankie Thomas (Tommy), Moroni Olsen (The Warden), Margot Stevenson (Sue), Marc Lawrence (Lefty), Joseph Downing (Johnny), Leo Gorcey (Jimmy), William Haade (Shrank), Tully Marshall (Old Peter).

Virginia City (1940)

Warner Bros. – First National. Director: Michael Curtiz. Executive producer: Hal B. Wallis. Associate producer: Robert Fellows. Screenplay by Robert Buckner (uncredited additional material by Howard Koch and Norman Reilly Raine). Music: Max Steiner. Photographed by Sol Polito. Art director: Ted Smith. Editor: George Amy. 121 minutes. Reno and Virginia City premiere: 16 March. With Errol Flynn (Kerry Bradford), Miriam Hopkins (Julia Hayne), Randolph Scott (Capt. Vance Irby), Humphrey Bogart (John Murrell), Frank McHugh (Mr. Upjohn), Alan Hale

(Moose), Guinn 'Big Boy' Williams (Marblehead), John Litel (Marshall), Douglass Dumbrille (Major Drewery), Moroni Olsen (Dr. Cameron), Russell Hicks (Armistead), Dickie Jones (Cobby Gill), Frank Wilcox (Union Soldier), Russell Simpson (Gaylord), Victor Kilian (Abraham Lincoln), Charles Middleton (Jefferson Davis), George Regas and Paul Fix (Murrell's henchmen), Ward Bond (Sergeant).

It All Came True (1940)

Warner Bros. – First National. Director: Lewis Seiler. Executive producer: Hal B. Wallis. Associate producer: Mark Hellinger. Screenplay by Michael Fessier and Lawrence Kimble, based on the novel *Better Than Life* by Louis Bromfield. Music: Heinz Roemheld. Photographed by Ernest Haller. Art director: Max Parker. Editor: Thomas Richards. Ninety-seven minutes. New York premiere: 5 April. With Ann Sheridan (Sarah Jane Ryan), Jeffrey Lynn (Tommy Taylor), Humphrey Bogart (Grasselli, alias Chips Maguire), Zasu Pitts (Miss Flint), Una O'Connor (Maggie Ryan), Jessie Busley (Mrs. Taylor), John Litel (Mr. Roberts), Grant Mitchell (Rene Salmon), Felix Bressart (The Great Boldini), Charles Judels (Henri Pepi de Bordeaux), Brandon Tynan (Mr. Van Diver), Howard Hickman (Mr. Prendergast), Herbert Vigran (Monks).

Brother Orchid (1940)

Warner Bros. – First National. Director: Lloyd Bacon. Executive producer: Hal B. Wallis. Associate producer: Mark Hellinger. Screenplay by Earl Baldwin, based on a magazine story by Richard Connell. Music: Heinz Roemheld. Photographed by Tony Gaudio. Art director: Max Parker. Editor: William Holmes. Ninety-one minutes. New York premiere: 7 June. With

Edward G. Robinson (Little John Sarto), Ann Sothern (Flo Addams), Humphrey Bogart (Jack Buck), Donald Crisp (Brother Superior), Ralph Bellamy (Clarence Fletcher), Allen Jenkins (Willie the Knife), Charles D. Brown (Brother Wren), Cecil Kellaway (Brother Goodwin), Morgan Conway (Philadelphia Powell), Richard Lane (Mugsy O'Day), Paul Guilfoyle (Red Martin), John Ridgely (Texas Pearson), Joseph Crehan (Brother MacEwen), Wilfred Lucas (Brother Mac-Donald), Tom Tyler (Curley Matthews), Dick Wessel (Buffalo Burns), Granville Bates (Pattonsville Supt.), Paul Phillips (French Frank), Don Rowan (Al Muller), Nanette Vallon (Fifi), Tim Ryan (Turkey Maloney), Joe Caites (Handsome Harry), Pat Gleason (Dopey Perkins), Tommy Baker (Joseph).

They Drive By Night (1940) (in Great Britain: **The Road to Frisco**)

Warner Bros. – First National. Director: Raoul Walsh. Executive producer: Hal B. Wallis. Associate producer: Mark Hellinger. Screenplay by Jerry Wald and Richard Macaulay, based on the novel *Long Haul* by A.I. Bezzerides. Music: Adolph Deutsch. Photographed by Arthur Edeson. Art director: John Hughes. Editor: Thomas Richards. Ninety-seven minutes. New York premiere: July. With George Raft (Joe Fabrini) Ann Sheridan (Cassie Hartley), Ida Lupino (Lana Carlsen), Humphrey Bogart (Paul Fabrini), Gale Page (Pearl Fabrini), Alan Hale (Ed Carlsen), Roscoe Karns (Irish McGurn), John Litel (Harry McNamara), George Tobias (George Rondolos), Henry O'Neill (District Attorney), Charles Halton (Farnsworth), Paul Hurst (Pete Haig), John Ridgely (Hank Dawson), George Lloyd (Barney), Joyce Compton (Sue Carter), Vera Lewis (Landlady), John Hamilton (Defense Attorney), Charles Wilson (Mike Williams), Norman Willis (Neves).

High Sierra (1941)

Warner Bros. – First National. Director: Raoul Walsh. Executive producer: Hal B. Wallis. Associate producer: Mark Hellinger. Screenplay by John Huston and W.R. Burnett, based on the latter's novel. Music: Adolph Deutsch. Photographed by Tony Gaudio. Art director: Ted Smith. Editor: Jack Killifer. 100 minutes. Los Angeles premiere: 23 January. With Ida Lupino (Marie), Humphrey Bogart (Roy Earle), Alan Curtis (Babe), Arthur Kennedy (Red), Joan Leslie (Velma), Henry Hull (Doc Banton), Henry Travers (Pa), Elizabeth Risdon (Ma), Jerome Cowan (Healy), Minna Gombell (Mrs. Baughman), Barton MacLane (Jack Kranmer), Cornel Wilde (Louis Mendoza), Donald MacBride (Big Mac), Paul Harvey (Mr. Baughman), Isabel Jewell (The Blonde), Willie Best (Algernon), Spencer Charters (Ed), George Meeker (Pfiffer), Robert Strange (Art), John Eldredge (Lon Preiser), Sam Hayes (Announcer), Louis Jean Heydt (Held-up hotel guest), Harry Hayden (Held-up storekeeper), Zero (Pard, the dog).

The Wagons Roll at Night (1941)

Warner Bros. – First National. Director: Ray Enright. Associate producer: Harlan Thompson. Screenplay by Fred Niblo Jr. and Barry Trivers, based on a story [the novel *Kid Galahad*] by Francis Wallace. Music: H. Roemheld. Photographed by Sid Hickox. Art director: Hugh Reticker. Editor: Mark Richards. Eighty-four minutes. Los Angeles premiere: 8 May. With Humphrey Bogart (Nick Coster), Sylvia Sidney (Flo Lorraine), Eddie Albert (Matt Varney), Joan Leslie (Mary Coster), Sig Rumann (Hoffman the Great), Cliff Clark (Doc), Charley Foy (Snapper), Frank Wilcox (Tex), John Ridgely (Arch), Clara Blandick (Mrs Williams), Aldrich Bowker (Mr. Williams), Garry

Owen (Gus), Jack Mower (Bundy), Frank Mayo (Wally).

The Maltese Falcon (1941)

Warner Bros. – First National. Director and screenplay: John Huston, based on the novel by Dashiell Hammett. Executive producer: Hal B. Wallis. Associate producer: Henry Blanke. Music: Adolph Deutsch. Photographed by Arthur Edeson. Art director: Robert Haas. Editor: Thomas Richards. 100 minutes. New York premiere: 3 October. With Humphrey Bogart (Sam Spade), Mary Astor (Brigid O'Shaughnessy), Gladys George (Iva Archer), Peter Lorre (Joel Cairo), Barton MacLane (Lt. Dundy), Lee Patrick (Effie Perine), Sydney Greenstreet (Kaspar Gutman), Ward Bond (Detective Tom Polhaus), Jerome Cowan (Miles Archer), Elisha Cook Jr. (Wilmer Cook), James Burke (Luke), Murray Alper (Frank Richman), John Hamilton (District Attorney Bryan), Walter Huston (Capt. Jacobi), Emory Parnell (Mate of La Paloma).

All Through the Night (1942)

Warner Bros. – First National. Director: Vincent Sherman. Associate producer: Jerry Wald. Screenplay by Leonard Spigelgass and Edwin Gilbert, based on a story by Leonard Spigelgass and Leonard Q. Ross. Music: Adolph Deutsch. Photographed by Sid Hickox. Art director: Max Parker. Editor: Rudi Fehr. 107 minutes. New York premiere: January. With Humphrey Bogart (Alfred 'Gloves' Donahue), Conrad Veidt (Ebbing), Kaaren Verne (Leda Hamilton), Jane Darwell (Ma Donahue), Frank McHugh (Barney), Peter Lorre (Pepi), Judith Anderson (Madame), William Demarest (Sunshine), Jackie C. Gleason (Starchie), Phil Silvers (Waiter), Wallace Ford (Spats Hunter), Barton MacLane (Marty Callahan), Edward

Brophy (Joe Denning), Martin Kosleck (Steindorff), Jean Ames (Annabelle), Ludwig Stossel (Mr. Miller), Irene Seidner (Mrs. Miller), James Burke (Forbes), Ben Welden (Smitty), Hans Schumm (Anton), Charles Cane (Spence), Frank Sully (Sage), Sam McDaniel (Deacon), Emory Parnell (Waterfront cop).

In This Our Life (1942)

Reputed guest appearance. New York premiere: 8 May.

The Big Shot (1942)

Warner Bros. – First National. Director: Lewis Seiler. Producer: Walter MacEwen. Screenplay by Bertram Millhauser, Abem Finkel and Daniel Fuchs. Music: Adolph Deutsch. Photographed by Sid Hickox. Art director: John Hughes. Editor: Jack Killifer. Eighty-two minutes. New York premiere: July. With Humphrey Bogart (Joseph 'Duke' Berne), Irene Manning (Lorna Fleming), Richard Travis (George Anderson), Susan Peters (Ruth Carter), Stanley Ridges (Martin Fleming), Minor Watson (Warden Booth), Chick Chandler (Dancer), Joseph Downing (Frenchy), Howard da Silva (Sandor), Murray Alper (Quinto), Roland Drew (Faye), John Ridgely (Tim), Joseph King (Toohey), John Hamilton (Judge), Virginia Brissac (Mrs. Booth), William Edmunds (Sarto), Virginia Sale (Mrs. Miggs), Ken Christy (Kat), Wallace Scott (Rusty), Ray Teal (Motorcycle cop).

Across the Pacific (1942)

Warner Bros. – First National. Director: John Huston. Producers: Jerry Wald and Jack Saper. Screenplay by Richard Macaulay, based on the story *Aloha Means Goodbye* by Robert Carson. Music: Adolph Deutsch.

Photographed by Arthur Edeson. Art directors: Robert Haas and Hugh Reticker. Editor: Frank Magee. Ninety-seven minutes. New York premiere: 4 September. With Humphrey Bogart (Rick Leland), Mary Astor (Alberta Marlow), Sydney Greenstreet (Dr. Lorenz), Charles Halton (A.V. Smith), Victor Sen Yung (Joe Totsuiko), Roland Got (Sugi), Lee Tung Foo (Sam Wing On), Frank Wilcox (Capt. Morrison), Paul Stanton (Col. Hart), Lester Matthews (Canadian Major), Roland Drew (Capt. Harkness), Monte Blue (Dan Morton), Kam Tong (T. Oki), John Hamilton (Court-Martial President), Tom Stevenson (Unidentified man), Chester Gan (Capt. Higoto), Richard Loo (First Officer Miyuma), Keye Luke (Steamship Office Clerk), Spencer Chan (Chief Engineer Mitsudo), Rudy Robels (Filipino assassin), Frank Faylen (Toy salesman), Tony Caruso (Cab driver).

Casablanca (1942)

Warner Bros. – First National. Director: Michael Curtiz. Producer: Hal B. Wallis. Screenplay by Julius J. and Philip G. Epstein and Howard Koch (also, uncredited, Casey Robinson), based on the play *Everybody Comes to Rick's* by Murray Burnett and Joan Alison. Music: Max Steiner. Photographed by Arthur Edeson. Art director: Carl Jules Weyl. Editor: Owen Marks. 102 minutes. New York premiere: November. With Humphrey Bogart (Rick Blaine), Ingrid Bergman (Ilsa Lund), Paul Henreid (Victor Laszlo), Claude Rains (Capt. Louis Renault), Conrad Veidt (Major Heinrich Strasser), Sydney Greenstreet (Señor Ferrari), Peter Lorre (Ugarte), S.Z. Sakall (Carl), Madeleine LeBeau (Yvonne), Dooley Wilson (Sam), John Qualen (Berger), Leonid Kinsky (Sacha), Joy Page (Annina Brandel), Helmut Dantine (Jan), Curt Bois (Pickpocket), Marcel Dalio (Emil, the Croupier), Corinna Mura (Singer), Ludwig Stossel (Mr. Leuchtag), Ilka Gruning (Mrs. Leuchtag), Charles La Torre (Capt. Tonelli), Frank Puglia (Arab vendor), Dan Seymour (Abdul).

Action in the North Atlantic (1943)

Warner Bros. – First National. Director: Lloyd Bacon. Producer: Jerry Wald. Screenplay by John Howard Lawson (additional dialogue by A.I. Bezzerides and W.R. Burnett), based on the novel by Guy Gilpatric. Music: Adolph Deutsch. Photographed by Ted McCord. Art director: Ted Smith. Editor: George Amy. 127 minutes. New York premiere: May. With Humphrey Bogart (Joe Rossi) Raymond Massey (Capt. Steve Jarvis), Alan Hale ('Boats' O'Hara), Julie Bishop (Pearl), Ruth Gordon (Sara Jarvis), Sam Levene ('Chips' Abrams), Dane Clark (Johnny Pulaski), Peter Whitney (Whitey Lara), Charles Trowbridge (Rear Admiral Hartridge), J.M. Kerrigan (Caviar Jinks), Dick Hogan (Cadet Robert Parker), Kane Richmond (Ensign Wright), Don Douglas (Lt. Commander), Ludwig Stossel (Capt. Ziemer), Iris Adrian (Jenny O'Hara).

Thank Your Lucky Stars (1943)

Guest appearance. New York premiere: 1 October.

Sahara (1943)

Columbia. Director: Zoltan Korda. Screenplay: John Howard Lawson and Zoltan Korda (adaptation by James O'Hanlon), from a screen story by Philip MacDonald based on an incident in the 1937 Soviet film *Trinadtsat* (*The Thirteen*) by Mikhail Romm. Music: Miklos Rozsa. Photographed by Rudolph Maté. Art directors: Lionel Banks and Eugene Lourié. Editor: Charles Nelson. Ninety-seven minutes. Premiere:

mid-October. With Humphrey Bogart (Sgt. Joe Gunn), Bruce Bennett (Waco Hoyt), J. Carroll Naish (Giuseppe), Lloyd Bridges (Fred Clarkson), Rex Ingram (Sgt.-Major Tambul), Richard Nugent (Capt. Halliday), Dan Duryea (Jimmy Doyle), Patrick O'Moore (Ozzie Bates), Carl Harbord (Marty Williams), Louis Mercier (Jean Leroux), Guy Kingsford (Peter Stegman), Kurt Kreuger (Capt. Von Schletow), John Wengraf (Major Von Falken), Hans Schumm (Sgt. Krause).

Passage to Marseille (1944)

Warner Bros. – First National. Director: Michael Curtiz. Producer: Hal B. Wallis. Screenplay by Casey Robinson and Jack Moffitt, based on the novel *Men Without A Country* by Charles Nordhoff and James Norman Hall. Music: Max Steiner. Photographed by James Wong Howe. Art director: Carl Jules Weyl. Editor: Owen Marks. 109 minutes. New York premiere: 16 February. With Humphrey Bogart (Jean Matrac), Claude Rains (Capt. Freycinet), Michéle Morgan (Paula), Philip Dorn (Renault), Sydney Greenstreet (Major Duval), Peter Lorre (Marius), George Tobias (Petit), Helmut Dantine (Garou), John Loder (Manning), Victor Francen (Capt. Malo), Vladimir Sokoloff (Grand-pére), Eduardo Ciannelli (Chief Engineer), Corinna Mura (Singer), Konstantin Shayne (First Mate), Stephen Richards [later Mark Stevens] (Lt. Hastings), Charles La Torre (Lt. Lenoir), Hans Conried (Jourdain), Monte Blue (Second Mate), Billy Roy (Mess Boy), Frederick Brunn (Bijou), Louis Mercier (Second Engineer).

Report from the Front (1944)

(Warner Bros.) American Red Cross. Director: Peter Godfrey. Screenplay by Mary McCall Jr. Premiere: 23 March. With Humphrey Bogart.

To Have and Have Not (1944)

Warner Bros. – First National. Director and producer: Howard Hawks. Screenplay by Jules Furthman and William Faulkner, based on the novel by Ernest Hemingway. Photographed by Sidney Hickox. Art director: Charles Novi. Editor: Christian Nyby. 100 minutes. New York premiere: 11 October. With Humphrey Bogart (Harry Morgan), Walter Brennan (Eddie 'The Rummy'), Lauren Bacall (Slim), Dolores Moran (Helène de Bursac), Hoagy Carmichael (Crickett), Walter Molnar (Paul de Bursac), Sheldon Leonard (Lieutenant Coyo), Marcel Dalio (Frenchy), Walter Sande (Johnson), Dan Seymour (Captain Renard), Aldo Nadi (Bodyguard), Paul Marion (Beauclerc), Patricia Shay (Mrs. Beauclerc), Pat West (Bartender), Emmett Smith (Emil).

Conflict (1945)

Warner Bros. – First National. Director: Curtis Bernhardt. Producer: William Jacobs. Screenplay by Arthur T. Horman and Dwight Taylor, based on a story by Robert Siodmak and Alfred Neumann. Music: Frederick Hollander. Photographed by Merritt Gerstad. Art director: Ted Smith. Editor: David Weisbart. Eighty-six minutes. New York premiere: June. With Humphrey Bogart (Richard Mason), Alexis Smith (Evelyn Turner), Sydney Greenstreet (Dr. Mark Hamilton), Rose Hobart (Kathryn Mason), Charles Drake (Prof. Norman Holdsworth), Grant Mitchell (Dr. Grant), Patrick O'Moore (Det. Lt. Egan), Ann Shoemaker (Nora Grant), Frank Wilcox (Robert Freston), Ed Stanley (Phillips), James Flavin (Det. Lt. Workman), Leah Baird (Martha Hamilton), Mary Servoss (Mrs. Allman), Wallis Clark (Writing Expert), Harlan Briggs (pawnshop clerk – second visit).

Hollywood Victory Caravan (1945)

War Activities Committee – U.S. Treasury Dept. –
Paramount. Director: William Russell. Script: Melville
Shavelson. Twenty minutes. (Bogart made a guest
appearance in this propaganda short promoting
Victory Loan bonds.)

Two Guys from Milwaukee (1946)

Guest appearance with Lauren Bacall. New York
premiere: July.

The Big Sleep (1946)

Warner Bros. – First National. Director and producer:
Howard Hawks. Screenplay by William Faulkner,
Leigh Brackett and Jules Furthman, based on the
novel by Raymond Chandler. Music: Max Steiner.
Photographed by Sid Hickox. Art director: Carl Jules
Weyl. Editor: Christian Nyby. 114 minutes. New York
premiere: 26 August. With Humphrey Bogart (Philip
Marlowe), Lauren Bacall (Vivian Rutledge), John
Ridgely (Eddie Mars), Martha Vickers (Carmen),
Dorothy Malone (Bookstore proprietress), Peggy
Knudsen (Mona Mars), Regis Toomey (Bernie Ohls),
Charles Waldron (General Sternwood), Charles D.
Brown (Norris), Bob Steele (Canino), Elisha Cook Jr.
(Harry Jones), Louis Jean Heydt (Joe Brody), Sonia
Darrin (Agnes), Theodore von Eltz (Arthur Geiger),
Tom Rafferty (Carol Lundgren), Joy Barlowe (Taxicab
driver), Tom Fadden (Sidney), Ben Welden (Pete),
Trevor Bardette (Art Huck), Joseph Crehan (Medical
Examiner).

Never Say Goodbye (1946)

Voice contribution. New York premiere: November.

Dead Reckoning (1947)

Columbia. Director: John Cromwell. Producer: Sidney Biddell. Screenplay by Oliver H.P. Garrett and Steve Fisher (adaptation by Allen Rivkin), based on a story by Gerald Adams and Sidney Biddell. Music: Marlin Skiles. Photographed by Leo Tover. Art directors: Stephen Goosson and Rudolph Sternad. Editor: Gene Havlick. 100 minutes. With Humphrey Bogart (Rip Murdock), Lizabeth Scott (Coral Chandler), Morris Carnovsky (Martinelli), Charles Cane (Lt. Kincaid), William Prince (Johnny Drake), Marvin Miller (Krause), Wallace Ford (McGee), James Bell (Father Logan), George Chandler (Louis Ord), William Forrest (Lt. Col. Simpson), Ruby Dandridge (Hyacinth).

The Two Mrs. Carrolls (1947)

Warner Bros. – First National. Director: Peter Godfrey. Producer: Mark Hellinger. Screenplay by Thomas Job, based on the play by Martin Vale. Music: Franz Waxman. Photographed by Peverell Marley. Art director: Anton Grot. Editor: Frederick Richards. Ninety-nine minutes. New York premiere: April. With Humphrey Bogart (Geoffrey Carroll), Barbara Stanwyck, (Sally), Alexis Smith (Cecily Latham), Nigel Bruce (Dr. Tuttle), Isobel Elsom (Mrs. Latham), Patrick O'Moore (Charles Pennington), Ann Carter (Beatrice Carroll), Anita Bolster (Christine), Barry Bernard (Blagdon), Colin Campbell (MacGregor), Peter Godfrey (First Racetrack Tout), Creighton Hale (Second Tout).

Dark Passage (1947)

Warner Bros. – First National. Director and screenplay: Delmer Daves, based on the novel by David Goodis. Producer: Jerry Wald. Music: Franz Waxman. Photographed by Sid Hickox. Art director: Charles H.

Clarke. Editor: David Weisbart. 106 minutes. New York premiere: September. With Humphrey Bogart (Vincent Parry), Lauren Bacall (Irene Jansen), Bruce Bennett (Bob), Agnes Moorehead (Madge Rapf), Tom D'Andrea (Sam, the Cabby), Clifton Young (Baker), Douglas Kennedy (Detective Kennedy), Rory Mallinson (George Fellsinger), Houseley Stevenson (Dr. Walter Coley).

Always Together (1947)

Guest appearance. New York premiere: December.

The Treasure of the Sierra Madre (1948)

Warner Bros. – First National. Director and screenplay: John Huston, based on the novel by B. Traven. Producer: Henry Blanke. Music: Max Steiner. Photographed by Ted McCord. Art director: John Hughes. Editor: Owen Marks. 126 minutes. Los Angeles premiere: January. With Humphrey Bogart (Fred C. Dobbs), Walter Huston (Howard), Tim Holt (Curtin), Bruce Bennett (Cody), Barton MacLane (McCormick), Alfonso Bedoya (Gold Hat), A. Soto Rangel (Presidente), Manuel Donde (El Jefe), Jose Torvay (Pablo), Margarito Luna (Pancho), Jacqueline Dalya (Flashy Girl), Bobby Blake (Mexican Boy), John Huston (Man in the White Suit), Harry Vejar (Bartender).

Key Largo (1948)

Warner Bros. – First National. Director: John Huston. Producer: Jerry Wald. Screenplay by Richard Brooks and John Huston, based on the play by Maxwell Anderson. Music: Max Steiner. Photographed by Karl Freund. Art director: Leo K. Kuter. Editor: Rudi Fehr. 101 minutes. New York premiere: 16 July. With Humphrey Bogart (Frank McCloud), Edward G.

Robinson (Johnny Rocco), Lauren Bacall (Nora Temple), Lionel Barrymore (James Temple), Claire Trevor (Gaye Dawn), Thomas Gomez (Curly Hoff), Harry Lewis (Toots Bass), John Rodney (Deputy Sawyer), Marc Lawrence (Ziggy), Dan Seymour (Angel), Monte Blue (Sheriff Ben Wade), Jay Silverheels and Rodric Red Wing (Osceola Brothers).

Knock On Any Door (1949)

Santana – Columbia. Director: Nicholas Ray. Producer: Robert Lord. Associate producer: Henry S. Kesler. Screenplay by Daniel Taradash and John Monks Jr., based on the novel by Willard Motley. Music: George Antheil. Photographed by Burnett Guffey. Art director Robert Peterson. Editor: Viola Lawrence. 100 minutes. New York premiere: February. With Humphrey Bogart (Andrew Morton), John Derek (Nick Romano), George Macready (Kerman, District Attorney), Allene Roberts (Emma), Susan Perry (Adele Morton), Mickey Knox (Vito), Barry Kelley (Judge Drake), Cara Williams (Nelly), Jimmy Conlin ('Kid Fingers' Conahan), Sumner Williams (Jimmy), Sid Molton (Squint), Pepe Hern (Juan), Dewey Martin (Butch), Robert A. Davis (Sunshine), Houseley Stevenson (Junior), Vince Barnett (Bartender), Thomas Sully (Officer Hawkins), Florence Auer (Aunt Lena), Pierre Watkin (Purcell), Gordon Nelson (Corey), Argentina Brunetti (Ma Romano), Dick Sinatra (Julian Romano), Carol Coombs (Ang Romano), Joan Baxter (Maria Romano).

Tokyo Joe (1949)

Santana – Columbia. Director: Stuart Heisler. Producer: Robert Lord. Associate producer: Henry S. Kesler. Screenplay by Cyril Hume and Bertram Millhauser (adaptation by Walter Doniger), based on a story by Steve Fisher. Music: George Antheil. Photographed by Charles Lawton Jr. Art director: Robert Peterson. Editor: Viola Lawrence. Eighty-eight minutes. New York premiere: 26 October. With Humphrey Bogart (Joe Barrett), Alexander Knox (Mark Landis), Florence Marly (Trina), Sessue Hayakawa (Baron Kimura Danshaku), Jerome Courtland (Danny), Gordon Jones (Idaho), Teru Shimada (Ito), Howard Kumagai (Kanda), Charles Meredith (General Ireton), Rhys Williams (Intelligence Officer), Lora Lee Michel (Anya), Gene Gondo (Supercargo), Whit Bissell (Clerk in charge of forms), Fred Sears (Doctor), Julia Fukuzaki (Maid), Hugh Beaumont (Passport control), Tommy Bond (Sergeant), Harlan Warde (Passport clerk on telephone), David Wolfe (Passport photographer).

Chain Lightning (1950)

Warner Bros. – First National. Director: Stuart Heisler. Producer: Anthony Veiller. Screenplay by Liam O'Brien and Vincent Evans, based on a story by J. Redmond Prior. Music: David Buttolph. Photographed by Ernest Haller. Art director: Leo K. Kuter. Editor: Thomas Reilly. Ninety-four minutes. Los Angeles premiere: 17 February. With Humphrey Bogart (Matt Brennan), Eleanor Parker (Jo Holloway), Raymond Massey (Leland Willis), Richard Whorf (Carl Troxell), James Brown (Major Hinkle), Roy Roberts (General Hewitt), Morris Ankrum (Bostwick), Fay Baker (Mrs. Willis), Fred Sherman (Jeb Farley).

In a Lonely Place (1950)

Santana – Columbia. Director: Nicholas Ray. Producer: Robert Lord. Associate producer: Henry S. Kesler. Screenplay by Andrew Solt (adaptation by Edmund H. North), based on a story by Dorothy B.

Hughes. Music: George Antheil. Photographed by Burnett Guffey. Art director: Robert Peterson. Editor: Viola Lawrence. Ninety-four minutes. New York premiere: May. With Humphrey Bogart (Dixon Steele), Gloria Grahame (Laurel Gray), Frank Lovejoy (Brub Nicolai), Carl Benton Reid (Capt. Lochner), Art Smith (Mel Lippman), Jeff Donnell (Sylvia Nicolai), Martha Stewart (Mildred Atkinson), Robert Warwick (Charlie Waterman), Morris Ankrum (Lloyd Barnes), William Ching (Ted Barton), Steven Geray (Paul), Hadda Brooks (Singer), Alice Talton (Frances Randolph), Jack Reynolds (Henry Kesler), Ruth Warren (Effie), Ruth Gillette (Martha), Guy Beach (Swan), Lewis Howard (Junior).

The Enforcer (1951) (in Great Britain: **Murder Inc.**)

United States – Warner Bros. Director: Bretaigne Windust (also, uncredited: Raoul Walsh). Producer: Milton Sperling. Screenplay by Martin Rackin. Music: David Buttolph. Photographed by Robert Burks. Art director: Charles H. Clarke. Editor: Fred Allen. Eighty-seven minutes. New York premiere: 25 January. With Humphrey Bogart (Martin Ferguson), Zero Mostel (Big Babe Lazich), Ted de Corsia (Joseph Rico), Everett Sloane (Albert Mendoza), Roy Roberts (Capt. Frank Nelson), Lawrence Tolan (James 'Duke' Malloy), King Donovan (Sgt. Whitlow), Robert (Bob) Steele (Herman), Adelaide Klein (Olga Kirshen), Don Beddoe (Thomas O'Hara), Tito Vuolo (Tony Vetto), John Kellogg (Vince), Jack Lambert (Philadelphia Tom Zaca), Patricia Joiner (Teresa Davis).

Sirocco (1951)

Santana – Columbia. Director: Curtis Bernhardt. Producer: Robert Lord. Associate producer: Henry S. Kesler. Screenplay by A.I. Bezzerides and Hans

Jacoby, based on the novel *Coup de Grâce* by Joseph Kessel. Music: George Antheil. Photographed by Burnett Guffey. Art director: Robert Peterson. Editor: Viola Lawrence. Ninety-eight minutes. London premiere: May. New York premiere: 13 June. With Humphrey Bogart (Harry Smith), Marta Toren (Violette), Lee J. Cobb (Col. Feroud), Everett Sloane (General LaSalle), Gerald Mohr (Major Leon), Zero Mostel (Balukjian), Nick Dennis (Nasir Aboud), Onslow Stevens (Emir Hassan), Ludwig Donath (Flophouse proprietor), David Bond (Achmet), Vincent Renno (Arthur), Martin Wilkins (Omar), Peter Ortiz (Major Robbinet), Edward Colmans (Col. Corville), Al Eben (Sergeant), Peter Brocco (Barber), Jay Novello (Hamal), Leonard Penn (Rifat), H. [Harry] Guardino (Lieut. Collet).

The African Queen (1951)

Romulus – Horizon – Independent through British Lion (Britain)/United Artists (U.S.A.). Director: John Huston. Producer: S.P. Eagle (Sam Spiegel). Screenplay by James Agee and John Huston (also, uncredited, Peter Viertel), based on the novel by C.S. Forester. Music: Allan Gray. Photographed by Jack Cardiff. Technicolor. Art director: Wilfred Shingleton. Editor: Ralph Kemplen. 103 minutes. Los Angeles premiere: 26 December. London premiere: 4 January 1952. With Humphrey Bogart (Charlie Allnut), Katharine Hepburn (Rose Sayer), Robert Morley (Rev. Samuel Sayer), Peter Bull (Captain of the Louisa), Theodore Bikel (First Officer – Louisa), Walter Gotell (Second Officer – Louisa), Gerald Onn (Petty Officer – Louisa), Peter Swanwick (First Officer – Shona Fort), Richard Marner (Second Officer – Shona Fort).

Deadline U.S.A. (1952) (in Great Britain: **Deadline**)

20th Century-Fox. Director and screenplay: Richard

Brooks. Producer: Sol C. Siegel. Music: Cyril Mockridge. Photographed by Milton Krasner. Art directors: Lyle Wheeler, George Patrick. Editor: William B. Murphy. Eighty-seven minutes. New York premiere: March. With Humphrey Bogart (Ed Hutchinson), Ethel Barrymore (Mrs. Garrison), Kim Hunter (Nora), Ed Begley (Frank Allen), Warren Stevens (George Burrows), Paul Stewart (Thompson), Martin Gabel (Rienzi), Joe De Santis (Herman Schmidt), Joyce MacKenzie (Kitty Garrison Geary), Audrey Christie (Mrs. Willebrandt), Fay Baker (Alice Garrison Courtney), Jim Backus (Cleary), Carleton Young (Crane), Selmer Jackson (Williams), Fay Roope (Judge), John Doucette (City News Editor), Raymond Greenleaf (Lawrence White), Tom Powers (Wharton), Philip Terry (Lewis Schaefer), Joe Sawyer (Whitey), Joseph Crehan (City Editor), Lawrence Dobkin (Hansen), Willis Bouchey (Henry), Paul Dubov (Dismissed employee).

U.S. Savings Bond Trailer (1952)

Metro–Goldwyn–Mayer. Release: 25 July. (Bogart promoted Series E Savings Bonds.)

Battle Circus (1953)

Metro–Goldwyn–Mayer. Director and screenplay: Richard Brooks, based on a story by Allen Rivkin and Laura Kerr. Producer: Pandro S. Berman. Music: Lennie Hayton. Photographed by John Alton. Art directors: Cedric Gibbons and James Basevi. Editor: George Boemler. Ninety minutes (in Great Britain: eighty-seven minutes). New York premiere: May. With Humphrey Bogart (Major Jed Webbe), June Allyson (Lt. Ruth McCara), Keenan Wynn (Sgt. Orville Statt), Robert Keith (Lt. Col. Whalters), William Campbell (Capt. John Rustford), Perry Sheehan (Lt. Laurence),

Patricia Tiernan (Lt. Rose Ashland), Adele Longmire (Lt. Jane Franklin), Jonathan Cott (Adjutant), Ann Morrison (Lt. Edith Edwards), Helen Winston (Lt. Graciano), Sarah Selby (Capt. Dobbs), Danny Chang (Danny), Philip Ahn (Korean Prisoner), Steve Forrest (Sergeant), Jeff Richards (Lieutenant), Dick Simmons (Capt. Norson).

Beat the Devil (1953)

Romulus – Santana – D.E.A.R. Film – Independent through British Lion (Great Britain)/United Artists (U.S.A.). Director: John Huston. Associate producer: Jack Clayton. Screenplay: Truman Capote (John Huston was also credited on American prints), based on the novel by James Helvick. Music: Franco Mannino. Photographed by Oswald Morris. Art director: Wilfred Shingleton. Editor: Ralph Kemplen. 100 minutes (Great Britain), ninety-two minutes (U.S.A). London premiere: November. New York premiere: 12 March 1954. With Humphrey Bogart (Billy Dannreuther), Jennifer Jones (Gwendolen Chelm), Gina Lollobrigida (Maria Dannreuther), Robert Morley (Peterson), Peter Lorre (Julius O'Hara), Edward Underdown (Harry Chelm), Ivor Barnard (Major Ross), Bernard Lee (Inspector Jack Clayton), Marco Tulli (Ravello), Mario Perroni (Purser), Alex Pochet (Manager – Hotel Bristol), Aldo Silvani (Charles), Giulio Donnini (Administrator), Saro Urzi (Captain), Juan de Landa (Hispano-Suiza Driver), Manuel Serano (Arab Officer), Mimo Poli (The Barman).

The Love Lottery (1954)

Guest appearance. London premiere: January.

The Caine Mutiny (1954)

Stanley Kramer – Columbia. Director: Edward Dmytryk. Producer: Stanley Kramer. Screenplay by Stanley Roberts (additional dialogue by Michael Blankfort), based on the novel by Herman Wouk, Music: Max Steiner. Photographed by Frank [Franz] Planer. Production designer: Rudolph Sternad. Art director: Cary Odell. Editors: William A. Lyon and Henry Batista. Technicolor. 125 minutes. New York premiere: 24 June. With Humphrey Bogart (Capt. Queeg), Jose Ferrer (Lt. Barney Greenwald), Van Johnson (Lt. Steve Maryk), Fred MacMurray (Lt. Tom Keefer), Robert Francis (Ensign Willie Keith), May Wynn (May Wynn), Tom Tully (Capt. DeVriess), E.G. Marshall (Lt. Cdr. Challee), Arthur Franz (Lt. Paynter), Lee Marvin (Meatball), Warner Anderson (Capt. Blakely), Claude Akins (Horrible), Katharine Warren (Mrs. Keith), Jerry Paris (Ensign Harding), Steve Brodie (Chief Budge), Todd Karns (Stilwell), Whit Bissell (Lt. Cdr. Dickson), James Best (Lt. Jorgensen), Joe Haworth (Ensign Carmody), Guy Anderson (Ensign Rabbit), James Edwards (Whittaker), Don Dubbins (Urban), David Alpert (Engstrand).

A Star Is Born (1954)

Voice contribution. Los Angeles premiere: September.

Sabrina (1954) (in Great Britain: **Sabrina Fair**)

Paramount. Director and producer: Billy Wilder. Screenplay by Billy Wilder, Samuel Taylor and Ernest Lehman, based on the play *Sabrina Fair* by Samuel Taylor. Music: Frederick Hollander. Photographed by Charles Lang Jr. Art directors: Hal Pereira and Walter Tyler. Editor: Arthur Schmidt. 114 minutes. London premiere: 10 September. New York Premier 22 September. With Humphrey Bogart (Linus Larrabee), Audrey Hepburn (Sabrina Fairchild), William Holden (David Larrabee), John Williams (Thomas Fairchild), Walter Hampden (Oliver Larrabee), Martha Hyer (Elizabeth Tyson), Joan Vohs (Gretchen Van Horn), Marcel Dalio (Baron), Marcel Hillaire (The Professor), Nella Walker (Maude Larrabee), Francis X. Bushman (Mr. Tyson), Ellen Corby (Miss McCardle), Marjorie Bennett (Margaret, the cook), Emory Parnell (Charles, the butler), Nancy Kulp (Jenny, the maid).

The Barefoot Contessa (1954)

Figaro – United Artists. Director and writer (also uncredited producer): Joseph L. Mankiewicz. Music: Mario Nascimbene. Photographed by Jack Cardiff. Art director: Arrigo Equini. Editor: William Hornbeck. Technicolor. 128 minutes. New York premiere: September. With Humphrey Bogart (Harry Dawes), Ava Gardner (Maria Vargas), Edmond O'Brien (Oscar Muldoon), Marius Goring (Alberto Bravano), Valentina Cortesa (Eleanora Torlato-Favrini), Rossano Brazzi (Vincenzo Torlato-Favrini), Elizabeth Sellars (Jerry Dawes), Warren Stevens (Kirk Edwards), Franco Interlenghi (Pedro), Mari Aldon (Myrna), Alberto Rabagliati (Night Club Proprietor), Tonio Selwart (The Pretender), Margaret Anderson (The Pretender's Wife), Bessie Love (Mrs. Eubanks), Enzo Staiola (Busboy), Maria Zanoli (Maria's mother), Renato Chiantoni (Maria's father), Bill Fraser (S. Montague Brown), John Parrish (Max Black), Jim Gerald (Mr. Blue), Diana Decker (Drunken blonde), Riccardo Rioli (Gypsy dancer), Gertrude Flynn (Lulu McGee), John Horne (Hector Eubanks), Robert Christopher (Eddie Blake), Anna Maria Paduan (Chambermaid), Carlo Dale (Chauffeur).

We're No Angels (1955)

Paramount. Director: Michael Curtiz. Producer: Pat Duggan. Screenplay by Ranald MacDougall, based on the play *La Cuisine des Anges* by Albert Husson. Music: Frederick Hollander. Photographed by Loyal Griggs. Art directors: Hal Pereira and Roland Anderson. Editor: Arthur Schmidt. Technicolor. VistaVision. 106 minutes. New York premiere: July. With Humphrey Bogart (Joseph), Aldo Ray (Albert), Peter Ustinov (Jules), Joan Bennett (Amelie Ducotel), Basil Rathbone (Andre Trochard), Leo G. Carroll (Felix Ducotel), Gloria Talbott (Isabelle Ducotel), John Baer (Paul Trochard), John Smith (Arnaud), Lea Penman (Madame Perone).

The Left Hand of God (1955)

20th Century–Fox. Director: Edward Dmytryk. Producer: Buddy Adler. Screenplay by Alfred Hayes, based on the novel by William E. Barrett. Music: Victor Young. Photographed by Franz Planer. Art directors: Lyle Wheeler and Maurice Ransford. Editor: Dorothy Spencer. Colour by DeLuxe. CinemaScope. Eighty-seven minutes. New York premiere: September. With Humphrey Bogart (Jim Carmody), Gene Tierney (Anne Scott), Lee J. Cobb (Mieh Yang), Agnes Moorehead (Beryl Sigman), E.G. Marshall (Dr. Sigman), Jean Porter (Mary Yin), Carl Benton Reid (Rev. Cornelius), Victor Sen Yung (John Wong), Philip Ahn (Jan Teng), Benson Fong (Chun Tien), Richard Cutting (Father O'Shea), Leon Lentok (Pao Ching), Don Forbes (Father Keller), Noel Toy (Woman in Sarong), Peter Chong (Feng – Merchant), Maria Tsien (Woman in Kimono), Stephen Wong (The Boy), Sophie Chin (Celeste), George Chan (Li Kwan), George Lee (Mi Lu), Stella Lynn (Pao Chu), Robert Burton (Rev. Martin), Soo Yong (Midwife).

The Desperate Hours (1955)

Paramount. Director and producer: William Wyler. Associate producer: Robert Wyler. Screenplay by Joseph Hayes, based on his novel and play. Music: Gail Kubik. Photographed by Lee Garmes. Art directors: Hal Pereira and Joseph MacMillan Johnson. Editor: Robert Swink. VistaVision. 112 minutes. New York premiere: October. With Humphrey Bogart (Glenn Griffin), Fredric March (Dan Hilliard), Arthur Kennedy (Jesse Bard), Martha Scott (Eleanor Hilliard), Dewey Martin (Hal Griffin), Gig Young (Chuck), Mary Murphy (Cindy Hilliard), Richard Eyer (Ralphie Hilliard), Robert Middleton (Kobish), Alan Reed (Detective), Bert Freed (Winston), Ray Collins (Masters), Whit Bissell (Carson), Ray Teal (Fredericks), Beverly Garland (Miss Swift), Walter Baldwin (Patterson).

The Harder They Fall (1956)

Columbia. Director: Mark Robson. Producer and screenplay: Philip Yordan, based on a novel by Budd Schulberg. Music: Hugo Friedhofer. Photographed by Burnett Guffey. Art director: William Flannery. Editor: Jerome Thoms. 109 minutes. New York premiere: May. With Humphrey Bogart (Eddie Willis), Rod Steiger (Nick Benko), Jan Sterling (Beth Willis), Mike Lane (Toro Moreno), Max Baer (Buddy Brannen), Jersey Joe Walcott (George), Edward Andrews (Jim Weyerhause), Harold J. Stone (Art Leavitt), Carlos Montalban (Luis Agrandi), Nehemiah Persoff (Leo), Felice Orlandi (Vince Fawcett), Herbie Faye (Max), Rusty Lane (Danny McKeogh), Jack Albertson (Pop), Val Avery (Frank), Tommy Herman (Tommy), Vinnie DeCarlo (Joey), Pat Comiskey (Gus Dundee), Matt Murphy (Sailor Rigazzo), Abel Fernandez (Chief Firebird), Marion Carr (Alice).

SELECT BIBLIOGRAPHY

Astor, Mary: *A Life on Film* (Delacorte, New York, 1971; W.H. Allen, London, 1973)

Bacall, Lauren: *By Myself* (Jonathan Cape, London, 1979)

Barbour, Alan G.: *Humphrey Bogart* (Pyramid Publications, New York, 1973)

Behlmer, Rudy: *Inside Warner Bros. (1935–1951)* (Viking, New York, 1986; Weidenfeld and Nicolson, London, 1986)

Benchley, Nathaniel: *Humphrey Bogart* (Hutchinson, London, 1975)

Bergman, Ingrid (with Alan Burgess): *My Story* (Michael Joseph, London, 1980)

Bronner, Edwin: *The Encyclopedia of the American Theatre 1900–1975* (A.S. Barnes, San Diego, 1980; Tantivy Press, London, 1980)

Brooks, Louise: *Lulu in Hollywood* (Hamish Hamilton, London, 1982)

Cagney, James: *Cagney by Cagney* (Doubleday, New York, 1976)

DiOrio Jr., Al: *Little Girl Lost* (Arlington House, New Rochelle, New York, 1973)

Gehman, Richard: *Bogart* (Gold Medal Books/Fawcett Publications, Greenwich, Connecticut, 1965; Oldbourne, London, 1967)

Geist, Kenneth L.: *Pictures Will Talk – The Life and Films of Joseph L. Mankiewicz* (Charles Scribner's Sons, New York, 1978; Frederick Muller, London, 1978)

Goldman, William: *Adventures in the Screen Trade* (Warner Books, New York, 1983; Macdonald, London, 1984)

Goodman, Ezra: *Bogey: The Good-Bad Guy* (Lyle Stuart, New York, 1965)

Higham, Charles: *Ava* (W.H. Allen, London, 1975)

Huston, John: *An Open Book* (Alfred A. Knopf, New York, 1980; Macmillan, London, 1981)

Hyams, Joe: *Bogie* (New American Library, New York, 1966; W.H. Allen, London, 1971)

Keyes, Evelyn: *Scarlett O'Hara's Younger Sister* (Lyle Stuart, Secaucus, New Jersey, 1977; W.H. Allen, London, 1978)

Koch, Howard: *As Time Goes By* (Harcourt Brace Jovanovich, New York and London, 1979)

McBride, Joseph: *Hawks on Hawks* (University of California Press, Berkeley/Los Angeles/London, 1982)

McCarty, Clifford: *Bogey – The Films of Humphrey Bogart* (Citadel Press, New York, 1965)

Massey, Raymond: *A Hundred Different Lives* (Robson Books, London, 1979)

Michael, Paul: *Humphrey Bogart – The Man and His Films* (Bobbs-Merrill, Indianapolis, 1965)

Pratley, Gerald: *The Cinema of John Huston* (Tantivy Press, London, 1977; A.S. Barnes, New Jersey, 1977)

Robinson, Edward G. (with Leonard Spigelgass): *All My Yesterdays* (Hawthorn Books, New York, 1973; W.H. Allen, London, 1974)

Ross, Lillian: *Picture* (Rinehart, New York, 1952)

Ruddy, Jonah, and Hill, Jonathan: *The Bogey Man – Portrait of a Legend* (Souvenir Press, London, 1965)

Thompson, Verita (with Donald Shepherd): *Bogie and Me* (St. Martin's Press, New York, 1982)

Wallis, Hal, and Higham, Charles: *Starmaker – the Autobiography of Hal Wallis* (Macmillan, New York, 1980)

Walsh, Raoul: *Each Man in His Time* (Farrar, Straus & Giroux, New York, 1974)

Warner, Jack L. (with Dean Jennings): *My First Hundred Years in Hollywood* (Random House, New York, 1964)

Warren, Douglas, with Cagney, James: *James Cagney — The Authorized Biography* (Robson Books, London, 1983)

Yablonsky, Lewis: *George Raft* (McGraw-Hill, New York, 1974; W.H. Allen, London, 1975)

Zolotow, Maurice: *Billy Wilder in Hollywood* (G.P. Putnam's Sons, New York, 1977; W.H. Allen, London, 1977)

Index

209

All Sphere Books are available at your bookshop or newsagent, or can be ordered from the following address: Sphere Books, Cash Sales Department, P.O. Box 11, Falmouth, Cornwall TR10 9EN

Please send cheque or postal order (no currency), and allow 60p for postage and packing for the first book plus 25p for the second book and 15p for each additional book ordered up to a maximum charge of £1.90 in U.K.

B.F.P.O. customers allow 60p for the first book, 25p for the second book plus 15p per copy for the next 7 books thereafter 9p per book.

Overseas customers, including Eire, please allow £1.25 for postage and packing for the first book, 75p for the second book and 28p for each subsequent title ordered.